Emotional Intelligence

The Mind-Blowing Dark Psychology Secrets to Be and Get What You Want.

By Alex Wallace

© COPYRIGHT 2019 - ALL RIGHTS RESERVED.

Emotional Intelligence

TABLE OF CONTENTS

Brain Rewire

**Manipulation and Persuasion
by NLP**

Brain Rewire

Cognitive behavioral therapy techniques made simple for retraining your conquering brain depression and anxiety

WHAT IS CBT?

When a person is diagnosed with depression and/or anxiety, most often it is because this individual has decided that he/she is no longer able to cope with the symptoms alone. Many people suffer in silence for years before someone suggests talking to someone about treatment. Many people live in denial, believing that they have everything under control and that they are just dealing with a lot of stress that they can't get away from.

Anxiety and depression are two of the most common mental illnesses in the Western world, and the treatment options vary according to each person's situation and a variety of factors, such as constitution, intensity and longevity of symptoms. Talk therapy is a form of treatment in which the patient comes in on a regular schedule to talk with a therapist in order to address the patient's mental health issues.

Mental illnesses like depression and anxiety carry a lot of stigma in Western society because, unlike other medically visible illnesses like cancer or cerebral palsy, you can't scan for depression or anxiety for a concrete picture of the problem. Many people totally unfamiliar with the struggles of those with depression might think that depression is just a person being really sad and that they just need to get over it and try harder to be happy. This is one of the most frustrating things for a depressed person to hear because the illness is actually a real medical condition that affects a person's ability to function and think clearly, depending on the severity.

Because of the fluidity of presentation when it comes to depression and anxiety, talk therapy treatments must be quite personalized and cater specifically to each person's problems. For this reason, talk therapy on a regular basis for a length of time gets pricey, as the therapist must make considerable efforts toward his/her patients to zero in on what makes them tick and progressively address each of the issues underlying their depression and anxiety symptoms.

Cognitive behavioral therapy is a common strategy for therapists who need to help a patient understand and address such issues. The therapy is a well-established practice that involves the patient in a big way. Contrary to a lot of people's idea of talk therapy, patients do not simply come in and lay on a couch to vent all of their problems and worries. Most talk therapy today, especially CBT, involves asking the patient to really get into their heads and their thought processes.

The trademark mechanic of depression and anxiety is a habitual pattern of negative thought or thoughts which perpetuate negative feelings like sadness, hopelessness, anger, or fear. It is these aggressively negative thought patterns that must be looked at closely, and not just run away from. The therapist acts as a guide for those who feel completely lost in their heads. Depression symptoms manifest in a variety of ways, and sometimes, the triggers underlying depression are not clear for each person. For anxiety sufferers, the triggers for such anxiety must be identified and addressed, as the feelings associated with this disorder appear in conjunction with the source of fear.

General Steps for CBT

CBT follows a sort of step-by-step process, the pace of which is dictated by the patient. One patient may need several weeks just to work out the situations and experiences in his life which are the source of depressive symptoms, while another patient may have a good handle on anxiety symptoms and simply need tools and strategies to help her cope with those specific situations. CBT is not just used for depression and anxiety sufferers. It works to help people through many different mental struggles, including PTSD, grief, medical illness, OCD, bipolar disorder, and even schizophrenia.

The first step in cognitive behavioral therapy is to identify thoroughly what it is in a person's life that is causing them stress. It could be a present situation or a distant memory. It could be a cumulative life experience that has led to a negative belief system or an acute, unexpected event which triggered their symptoms. This is arguably the most important step in CBT because many people develop habits which help them avoid or run away from the thoughts that cause them pain. This is why, as mentioned before, many people need a professional as a sort of guide but also as someone to help a patient remain accountable to the process and see himself through to the end in order to see real, visible improvement.

The truth is, however, anyone can apply these steps to their own lives in order to address problems and move toward a better place mentally. No one in this world is without experiences of pain in some form. If you have picked up this book, it is because you have either an interest in the therapy or a personal need that you are trying to address through CBT. I encourage you to take some time here as we discuss the steps of CBT to get out a journal and a pen and begin writing about yourself, your feelings, and your struggles. The first step in any and all forms of recovery is identifying and coming to terms with the situations, emotions, people, belief systems, experiences, memories, etc., that are triggering your feelings associated with depression and anxiety. Remember, although you can educate yourself and make informed decisions about whether you are clinically suffering from depression or anxiety, only a professional can make these official diagnoses for you.

If you were in your first appointment for CBT with a professional, you would begin by unloading lots of information, including your personal history and family history of mental or other illness. If you are following along in a journal, start by writing down whatever you can think of in terms of your personal history that may be relevant to the symptoms you are going through right now and trying to address. Do you have a mother who also suffered from depression? There is a genetic component to mental illness. Do you remember a traumatic incident in your childhood involving other members of your family? How long have you felt troubling feelings? Can you estimate how long you've experienced negative thought patterns?

As you start from your earliest memories associated with your present experience, gradually begin to work your way forward in time to where you are now. What are your best guesses as to why you feel the way you do? It may be clear as day or murky with lots of different factors influencing your moods, behaviors, or thought patterns. The point of this first step is to really unpack the thoughts, feelings and experiences which your subconscious mind may be trying to protect you from by hiding them, tucking them neatly away to be ignored. Sometimes bringing these up to the surface is a painful experience, and it is up to you to decide whether or not you're going to need support for this to happen effectively and fully. Sometimes we need support, and this is not something to be ashamed of. It doesn't mean you are weak or broken or a lost cause. Ask a friend or close family member to help you walk through those most painful experiences or thoughts if you need to.

The second step in the cognitive behavioral therapy process is to pinpoint the things you wish to work on through therapy specifically. Perhaps you have severe social anxiety and want to learn how to cope with this anxiety in order to leave the house and go to the grocery store or meet friends for dinner once in a while without feeling panicked. Come up with some concrete goals for yourself that you can see yourself accomplishing in your mind's eye. You may find it really hard to believe you can get there at the present moment, but can you visualize yourself waking up in the morning and smiling and feeling ready to face the day without those thought cycles digging in, telling you to stay in bed, that you are worthless, that you can't do anything helpful, etc.? Just visualizing yourself in a different scenario on a regular basis can start the process of changing your brain chemistry to focus on a new reality. Practice being an advocate for yourself.

In your journal, outline your personal goals in detail. Your brain will try to hit you relentlessly with thoughts telling you this is hopeless, why are you even trying, etc., but do your best to fight through those thoughts. Write down exactly where you would like to be after having addressed these issues and applied new coping strategies and tools.

The next step is probably the most painful for most patient suffering from depression and anxiety and involves becoming as aware as possible of yourself as you experience those emotions and feelings that plague your everyday life. The therapist will have the patient think about the situations or triggers for their depressive or anxious feelings and really engage with themselves at that moment. Where do the feelings start to surface? How intense do they get as you think about those troubling situations, feelings, or thought patterns? Where are they most intense? What feelings are evolving as you sit in that situation? What are the thoughts going through your mind? Is there a pattern of one or two thoughts which come up most frequently? Which thought patterns are most hurtful? Is there a point where you are compelled to recede and give up and go back to bed? Keep track of your answers to these questions as you write, if they apply to your personal situation. This exercise may also help you with the previous steps to pinpoint specific triggers and struggles to focus on.

The next step is to focus specifically on those

thought patterns and identify where your thinking is flawed. A lot of times, our minds do a great job of convincing us of a reality which supports those feelings keeping us down. We become addicted to the thought patterns and associated feelings, and this makes it feel almost impossible to break free. Know that this is not impossible and that these steps are taking you along a road of progress, even if you don't feel it yet. Coming to terms with thought patterns is such a big, important step. Let the clarity of your situation come forward as you stop running away. Ask yourself questions about these thought cycles, like, "How accurate is this belief system?" "Do I just think this way because I feel hurt?" "What evidence do I have that this feeling is justified?" etc.

The final step in CBT involves effortfully reshaping those thought patterns into new, more helpful thought patterns in order to dispel the associated emotional responses. You may be surprised to learn that the brain is actually capable of rewiring itself with habitual practice to form new thought patterns through a concept called "neuroplasticity." Each time you recognize a familiar thought process rising up to tear you down emotionally, you must counter this thought pattern with a new truth. Let's look at an example.

A girl who suffers from social anxiety may start feeling more and more anxious as a social event draws near. Thoughts like, "no one actually wants me here" or "you're going to do something embarrassing" might crop up. Instead of letting these thoughts get the best of her, she counters these thoughts with truths based in reality, such as, "I was specifically invited, and they said they were excited to see me" and "Can you think of a single situation in which something you did made your friends not want to be your friend? Everyone does silly things at parties once in a while." If she makes this a habit, she will find, over time, that those negative thought patterns are no longer automatic and habitual, and her new thought patterns will begin to take their place.

The History of CBT and How It Was Developed

Now that you've gotten a brief introduction to CBT and the steps involved, let's look briefly at how CBT evolved to its present form.

In the present use of cognitive behavioral therapy, the focus is placed firmly on how the sufferer is relating to his/her thought patterns in an effort adjust those associations to reflect reality and dispel inaccurate and hurtful thought cycles. But this wasn't always the focus.

Most of you reading this book have at least heard the name Freud. Freud is credited as one of the most influential and groundbreaking innovators responsible for new ideas of psychoanalysis. Though psychology has in large part moved on and away from some of his original thoughts, his work was very important in terms of the advancement of what we now recognize widely as talk therapy.

Different approaches to psychoanalysis include the psychodynamic, humanistic, and finally, cognitive. Our present practice of CBT is commonly referred to as the "third wave" of cognitive therapy and reflects developments and progress that we've seen evolving over the past decade. The world of psychology and talk therapy is constantly changing as we discover newer and better ways to help people deal with their unique struggles. And, just as the variability of specific needs is pretty much endless, the approaches and practices available today reflect our attempts to address the needs of a wide variety of patients.

What characterizes the third wave of cognitive behavioral therapy is a movement toward how a person relates to what they are thinking and feeling, whereas in earlier practice, the focus was given to changing behaviors. It used to be believed that it was bad behaviors which led to such painful and negative emotions and thought patterns, instead of behaviors arising as a response to them. Those suffering from depression who decide to self-medicate through alcohol consumption may have talked to a therapist decades ago who would have suggested that if she just stopped the drinking, the depression symptoms could be dispelled. Nowadays, we would more readily identify that the behavior is actually a result of hitting a wall when it came to dealing with a depression which seemed insurmountable. Drinking dulls the senses and the mind slows down, alleviating the symptoms of negative thought cycles temporarily.

As cognitive therapy has progressed, the focus has moved more and more toward a holistic, big-picture way of thinking about the sufferer's problems. We've moved away from the way of thinking that says, "you are fundamentally flawed, we are going to change and fix you" and toward a practice which emphasizes a more personal, subjective approach. What is important, in many third wave therapists' thinking, is that a person who is able to function and relate positively to the world and in his/her relationships. It's not a matter of prying out the bad thing living in your brain, but about understand it thoroughly, where it comes from, how it affects your current way of thinking, and how to adjust it to the betterment of yourself and your quality of life.

Principles of CBT Treatment

The core principles of CBT originate with the credited founder of the therapy, a practitioner named Aeron Beck, MD. His daughter, Judy Beck, went on to further his work and contribute her own important work to the development of CBT thought and practice. In her book, Cognitive Therapy: Basics and Beyond (1995), she outlines several core principles which hold to the core values of the therapy today and are important for understanding its unique use and effective application in today's talk therapy.

A couple of the most simple principles include that CBT is to be relatively short-term, and that the sessions should be structured. From the outset, CBT is about forming an action plan with a definite goal or set of goals in mind. The sufferer must pinpoint specific issues and triggers, causing unwanted thought cycles and emotions, then decide on specific things to focus on for the duration of therapy. The patient spends limited time ruminating and wandering and second-guessing and is constantly encouraged toward engagement, awareness and therapy in action. The course of CBT for an individual may last as little as five weeks up to around 20, in general.

Before getting started in this very important journey, it is essential in CBT that the patient is paired with a therapist with whom she gets along and feels comfortable. It can be a considerable hindrance to the effectiveness of therapy if a patient does not feel comfortable enough with his/her therapist to really open up in front of them. He may feel uncomfortable talking about one or two issues, and these may be the most important to address. Or she may feel embarrassed or vulnerable, being emotional and accessing her emotions fully with a certain therapist, limiting progress. So, at the outset, it is crucial that a good pairing is made and, if the patient does not feel comfortable, they should request or look for a different therapist. A lot of the time, it will simply come down to personality. Needing a different therapist does not necessarily mean that this one is "bad" or not as skilled. Some personalities and dispositions require a quieter, introverted personality in order to open up, while others may respond to someone who is more assertive and direct.

As mentioned before, CBT is not about laying back and letting a therapist talk at you and fix your problems for you. It requires a lot on the part of the patient, and if you are reading this with a determination to begin addressing your personal issues yourself, know that it can be an arduous road to follow. A therapist can be a powerful ally on this journey by serving as a consistent advocate and guide.

In our modern society, it is easier than ever to zone out and distract oneself on a near constant basis if he really wants to. From the moment we get up in the morning to going to bed at night, people are constantly taking in information on the go or at work or in front of their TVs at home. We don't necessarily have to take the time to be mindful or think about things on a deeper level if we don't want to. If we've got enough going in our lives, then these responsibilities can take over, and we can push things to the back of our minds that we don't want to deal with.

But eventually, a sufferer from conditions like anxiety and depression is going to reach a breaking point where the incessant pain and self-torture becomes too much. This is a critical point at which a person must choose how they are going to deal with the situation. If thinking about and addressing emotional issues seems too much, that person may choose to self-medicate through dangerous means or find other ways to continue running away. But depression can lead to a near complete inability to function. Many people find themselves so lethargic and hollow inside that they cannot even get themselves out of bed or perform mundane tasks like brushing their teeth or combing their hair. This is often recognized by others around the sufferer, and this person may be the catalyst for the sufferer to seek help.

Therapy like CBT can be a scary step simply because the obstacles seem insurmountable and the pain unbearable. But the only way to dispel such demons is to confront them head-on. No amount of ignoring is going to make the foundation of your negative emotions simply go away over time. But if done correctly and methodically, CBT can ease the sufferer into the process through baby steps and exercises in mindfulness that is always accompanied by a positive outlook that looks forward toward your goals.

It is important to note that not every mental health condition and situation is suited to a CBT strategy. Very complex mental conditions may require other forms of therapy or treatment instead of or in addition to CBT, and this can only be determined by a medical professional.

Expectations of Treatment

As with any form of talk therapy designed to treat a patient's mental and emotional issues, the outcome of the treatment is going to rely a great deal on what the client has put into it. It is important that a client is coming to therapy of his own free will and not because a family member or close friend is badgering them to go. It is not uncommon for a client who has been forced into therapy to walk into a room with a therapist and simply remain silent for the duration. This is an incredible waste of time and money, but most importantly, the client is not in the right mindset to begin making changes or addressing issues.

You can't force someone to utilize therapy effectively. But when a person decides to become an advocate for themselves and begin the process of helping themselves out of the painful emotional cycle they are experiencing; then they are well on the way to a successful therapy experience.

Take yourself, for example. If you are reading this book because you are ready to try and address the emotional circumstances in your life which you feel are holding you back or dragging you down in some way, then you are definitely advocating for your health and wellbeing. There are many techniques available for people to try on their own in an effort to address issues and make positive changes in their lives. Many of these techniques do not necessarily require a therapist to guide you through, though it is important to receive proper assessment if symptoms are severe and hindering your ability to function.

Most people in the world today suffer from some kind of emotional habit that makes them feel a certain negative way when something specific is triggered. Perhaps someone who grew up overweight feels a twinge of pain any time she hears someone make a comment about another fat person. This response makes sense logically, as a particularly painful memory is being triggered, and there follows a sad feeling. But if this thought pattern becomes chronic and associates with severe forms of self-abuse in the form of obsessive thoughts, talking at yourself, and feelings of worthlessness, then this woman may be heading quickly toward a depressive state, if she has not already arrived.

A person who recognizes this progression and decides to get help through CBT will realize that there is a negative thought pattern at work triggering these feelings. Someone who has internalized this feeling of inadequacy and sense of being flawed is not necessarily going to see a solution in the form of cognitive therapy because to them. Their flaw is simply a fact of life and something they cannot change. This is an important switch that needs to be made before progress can be made through CBT. A person must realize that their pain may be a result of a flawed pattern of thought, not an innate flaw within themselves.

It is impossible to cover all of the possibilities and situations in which CBT may come into play, but the important thing to note when considering expectations for therapy is that it takes active participation and willingness to engage with painful emotions on the part of the client. This is not an easy thing, and real self-improvement is never as easy as taking a pill or reading a book. But it is possible to retrain your brain to think in new and different ways that do no feed the relentless cycle of painful emotions and negative behaviors. The brain is ready and willing to form new habits. It just takes some dedication and consistency on the part of the patient to get there. In the end, whenever those troublesome triggers come up, your new strategies will help the patient redirect those once dominant thought patterns into new ones which are not connected with pain. In this way, painful emotional cycles are gradually alleviated as the individual begins to accept new truths about herself and her relationship with the world.

In the next chapter, we will look at several of the common mental and emotional disorders which can be addressed effectively through the implementation of cognitive behavioral therapy. The list is not exhaustive but will touch on many struggles which appear everywhere and every day in modern society. In many cases, some of the struggles are, in fact, a direct result of our modern society. Hopefully, as we learn more and more about human psychology and mental disorders, we will also learn to address those aspects of our social world, which prove more harmful than helpful.

If by the end of this book you feel you have learned

a great deal to the betterment of your life or the lives of your loved ones, please consider writing a positive review to share your experience with others who may benefit from this information.

Problems and Issues

The effectiveness of CBT is certainly not limited to anxiety and depression. It has been used to address and treat many disorders across a wide range of situations, and it is important to understand just why and how CBT has proven effective in all of these different arenas.

As with many mood disorders, it is important to understand that in general, emotions such as fear, anger, sadness, and happiness have their place in human biology and play a vital role in how we function and survive. Fear is essential for preparing the body for the fight or flight response when potential danger is near. Sadness and happiness are natural indicators that whatever activity we are engaging in is either good or bad for us. We feel good after eating a healthy meal or exercising, and we feel bad after eating too much sugar or starch.

It is when these emotional responses become chronically overstimulated and tied in with thought processes and behaviors that the trouble enters a person's life. Too much fear manifests as a phobia, too much sadness manifests as depression, too much worry, anxiety, etc. There is an important difference between someone with a chronic anxiety disorder and someone who simply worries a lot, and the language here is similar to that of a discussion on addiction. Let's zero in on worry as our first focus in a list of disorders CBT can address.

We are all familiar with feelings of worry, and a certain amount of it is perfectly appropriate and actually beneficial. It may not be a pleasant emotion, but it puts us on high alert so that our senses are heightened, and we are motivated to take necessary action to do what needs to be done in order to alleviate the sources of that worry.

Worry

Let's look at an example of worry on a normal scale, then examine what it might look like when worry turns to a detrimental source of stress and anxiety.

A mother helps her son pack his bags as he gets ready to move into a college dorm. It is a big step for any young man or woman, and there is a mixture of excitement and a little bit of anxiety about the future. The son gets ready to hug his mom goodbye, and his mom is in tears. It is a familiar sight on college campuses around the world as the beginning of a new school year approaches.

The mother may go home and continue to think about her son all evening, as she's making dinner, wondering how he's settling in, etc. She may have others in the family who are around her to comfort her. This is perfectly normal. But let's say that after a few months, she begins to have intrusive thoughts throughout the day which plant worries in her head which are unfounded. She suddenly has a thought while she's at work that her son might not have enough money to eat properly. Maybe he's eating junk and becoming unhealthy. The thought goes around and around in her mind until she absolutely must pick up her cell phone and call her son to make sure he's ok. On the phone, her son assures her that he is fine and making money at a part-time job to eat decent meals. The mother's mind rests…until that night.

She lies awake with other intrusive thoughts and worries springing to mind; what if he's engaged with his friends in parties that have drinking and drugs? What if he's in trouble right now? I had bad friends in college, what if he's being left somewhere alone? What if no one is there to help him? The worry escalates in her mind until she is in a near state of panic. She wants desperately to reach for her phone again and call her son, but it is the middle of the night. Somewhere in her mind, despite the cloud of worry that is overwhelming her, she knows that these thoughts and worries are disproportionate to reality. There is no reason for her to suddenly be afraid of these things, although because the possibility exists, it is very difficult to convince her brain that it is being irrational.

This level of anxiety and worry can get in the way to daily living and have an impact on overall health, factors which determine whether an emotion is normal or turning into a disorder. A lot of the time, with worry, the trouble with assuaging a person's fears has to do with the fact that there is the possibility that something is going wrong or that something bad is happening. It's just that they need to be convinced of the low probability. Certainly, there is the possibility every single day that something terrible is going to happen, but can you imagine if everybody lived out their lives with continuous fear and anxiety about those things happening? Worry is triggered and convinces the brain that something is not only possible but probable, almost inevitable. This is where cognitive behavioral therapy can be useful, especially if the individual is aware of that, although these feelings and emotions are very strong, they are also irrational. Once there have been steps toward an understanding of the emotion, a door may be opened toward changing the way one processes and relates to those fears.

The mom may take some time to herself and consider her emotions carefully. She knows that her worry stems from a deep love and concern for her son, but the specific fears she has concerning his wellbeing are conjured from thin air and without foundation in reality. Her first practical steps along the path of CBT to solve her problems would be to stay aware of herself and her emotions and the next time something triggers that worry, to take a step back and observe it objectively. Why am I having this thought? Where did it come from? What reason do I have to think this is happening? The more she engages with her thought processes, the more she can address them by questioning their validity, their origins, and then start replacing those thoughts with others that are founded in reality. Over time, bad habits of thought can turn to more positive, grounded thoughts.

Anger

If you've ever felt the heat of the moment when you are angry, which almost all of us have, you know that the idea of dispelling that anger in the moment seems quite difficult. Anger is a powerful emotion and one that often leads to actions and words which we may desperately regret later. Many people struggle with a level of irritability that has a very negative impact on their relationships. As with all other emotions, anger has a place in human biology and our evolution and survival. However, just like every other emotion, there is a possibility of anger becoming a habitual go-to emotion in times of stress where the emotion is disproportionate to the situation.

For example, anger can be useful if, say, a mother's babies are threatened by another creature and it is up to the mother to either defend her babies and fight away the threat or surrender. The behavior varies across different species, of course, but anger in this situation may be the only thing that saves the defenseless babies as the adrenaline coursing through the mom's veins give her motivation and strength to become strong and fight off a threat.

But anger can also become a bad habit, easily triggered by events and circumstances which do not seem to warrant the level of anger expelled by someone prone to it. Anger management is a common therapy treatment with a lot of aims and strategies in common with CBT. The individual must learn tools that he or she can use whenever their irrational anger is triggered. In extreme circumstances, this can mean the difference between calming down or moving toward physical behaviors in line with their emotional response, which may lead to violence against things or people. This disorder is much more prevalent in men, and it can be incredibly difficult to manage, oftentimes because the anger has been spurred on by past events which have hurt the individual in deep ways. It is quite common for violent criminals to cite past experiences of abuse when they think about their automatic and violent reactions of anger. Deep-seated pain as a result of hurt pride or embarrassment can feed resentment, making anger and frustration easily accessible anytime even minor upsets occur in the individual's life.

Though the challenge may seem insurmountable, CBT has been proven helpful in this arena as well. As with any therapy treatment, the results will depend largely on the efforts put forth by the individuals being treated. Tools and strategies for combatting irrational anger are going to be very important here, not only for the wellbeing of the sufferer but also of other potential victims in proximity to him.

Panic Attacks

Many people suffer from panic attacks brought on by various stimuli, which vary according to each person's struggles and experiences. Panic attacks are often comorbid conditions of anxiety disorders as well as other fear-based disorders, like phobia.

The experience of a panic attack can vary slightly from person to person but generally is described as a sudden, acute experience of fear that is accompanied by rapid heartbeat, irregular rapid breathing, and a general sense of helplessness in the face of their situation. Panic attacks can be triggered by already established fears or fears of the unknown. Severity and frequency vary across individuals, but the experience is always quite frightening and can be a devastating part of a person's life, as their fears are made to be even more burdensome as they dread the next panic attack they won't see coming.

CBT in this situation will work to address not only the triggers which set off the panic attacks but also the tools that can be used to work the way through the panic attack and then, over time, minimize their frequency over time.

Panic attacks are a result of a progressive line of thought that convinces the brain that there is a reason to be afraid. Panic attacks associated with social anxiety, for example, tend to develop from the belief that they are bringing undue attention to themselves and are about to suffer a devastatingly embarrassing event. Someone with acute anxiety triggered by other people may feel a panic attack rising just from the experience of someone looking at them too intently. Individuals who are autistic also often experience a tremendous amount of distress when someone tries to look at them in their eyes or for what feels like too long or too intensely. It can feel impossible to stop this process once it gets going, but there are strategies associated with CBT, which will work to dispel rising feelings of panic through engaging the mind in rational thought. The practitioner must ground themselves in their surroundings and counter their suspicions of danger with statements that reflect what is actually happening. The more he/she can do this, the more the process of panic will be effectively interrupted. Over time, this practice has proven to drastically reduce the frequency and potency of panic attacks in people who thought they could never be free of them.

Insomnia

Insomnia is characterized by a prolonged inability to fall asleep, which affects one's ability to function on an optimal level consistently over a long period of time. It is not uncommon for a person to find trouble sleeping every now and then, but the insomniac will have this experience on a chronic level, where lack of sleep is much more prevalent than nights where sleep is achieved. Unfortunately, insomniacs tend to develop habits of behavior which only serve to discourage the body to reach a restful state where it is ready for sleep. Individuals frustrated with their wakefulness might resign themselves to the couch to sit in front of a TV and watch movies all night, or they might play video games or read on their phones, etc. These activities essentially wake up the brain even more as the individual exposes themselves to light that the brain associates with waking hours. But these things are preferable to lying awake in bed for hours and hours.

CBT allied with addressing behaviors that will encourage the body to relax can go a long way in retraining the body for sleep. Many people will benefit from medication in conjunction with therapy, and results are going to vary quite a bit just because everyone's biology is different, especially when it comes to sleep disorders and how they have formed.

The body must relearn how to become restful, and behaviors like exposing the brain to bright light late into the night must be adjusted. Other behaviors that may be present and hindering sleep include eating late at night and engaging in wakeful activities in bed, like watching a movie on your iPad. Calming practices like mindfulness meditation may be helpful in ridding the mind of thought processes, especially if they are triggering anxiety and worry. Exercising in the afternoon so that the body is tired and ready to sleep by evening time is also a helpful tool. CBT may be necessary if the main thing keeping a person up at night is obsessive thought cycles. Addressing these issues during daytime CBT sessions and then focusing on calming habits and changing behavioral habits in the evening and at night may be effective when used together consistently.

Eating Disorders

Another terrifying disorder that has been on the rise in recent decades is the eating disorder. Eating disorders encompass all forms of disorders in which a person has an unhealthy relationship with food, which causes unhealthy behaviors in terms of eating. These disorders are intimately linked with a progressively strong conviction that the eating behavior is necessary because of a fear of becoming fat or obsession with control. Many young girls as young as 9 and 10 have been reported with eating disorders in response to a culture which values thinness and connects being thin with being beautiful. It's a message we've seen for years and years in the Western world and one which has a very strong grip on men and women of all ages today. The progression to an eating disorder may follow many different pathways, but almost always stems from a desire to change one's physical appearance from sub-par to what they perceive as attractive, ideal, or sexy. These demands may originate from a desire to be socially popular or a desire to excel in a skill or sport, among many other motivations. Some people are driven by a sense of control, and the ability to control something as powerful as hunger offers an intense high as they are able to withstand the temptation to eat, giving them a false sense of strength when in fact their bodies are suffering.

Anorexia and bulimia are two of the most common types of eating disorders. Anorexia involves an individual restricting food intake to the point where they lose massive amounts of weight and become frail, but still believing they are too big and need to keep restricting. Their view of their bodies becomes warped, and their belief system revolves around a fear of eating too much and becoming fat again. Bulimia is another strategy of control where a person will develop a dangerous cyclic habit of binging and purging in an effort to get rid of everything they take in. This behavior often results in many associated health risks, like damage to the esophagus and stomach, and is intertwined with a belief system that is not founded in reality.

The CBT approach in this situation is going to be incredibly important in terms of helping the client to become aware of her flawed patterns of thought. Her habitual believe system is going to be difficult to challenge because she's been supporting and fortifying this belief system with behavior which has given her results. These results, though detrimental to everyone else looking in from the outside, is going to feel like a victory and a strength in a very real way to the client. But she is also going to be aware of her body crying out for help because the body does a very good job of sending signals to let us know when something is wrong. All that needs to happen now is for the brain to let go of those false beliefs.

A CBT therapist may begin by presenting a series of facts to the sufferer regarding his/her health. Let's use a young teenage woman named Cindy as an example. Cindy present with years of anorexic behaviors behind her. She's lost a great deal of weight and at age 19 at the height of 5'6", she is under 100 lbs. The doctors may have told her over and over, as well as family and friends who care about her, that this is not healthy. Cindy knows deep down that this is probably not something she can continue doing forever, but she is unsure how to address what's going on.

As follows with the general principles of CBT, Cindy will be asked to analyze her thought patterns and find the root cause of this habitual behavior. Was she determined to lose weight initially because she felt she was unattractive? Is she trying to excel at a sport like running or gymnastics or basketball? Does she feel ugly and inadequate when she's not exercising this level of control over herself? The next questions might revolve around why she feels this way. This is going to be key in helping Cindy to realize that her beliefs are based on fantasy, on false hopes, or marketing ploys. Being too thin and without strength will never help her become a strong athlete. Her idea of beauty is the result of marketing and airbrushed images and an unattainable ideal. Her sense that she is worthless if she cannot control her weight is completely unfounded and may stem from some other circumstance in her life, which is out of her control and causing her anxiety or pain. Oftentimes, young adults will exercise dangerous control over their bodies or something else in an effort to counteract the fact that there is something else going on in their lives that is outside their control, such as a dying loved one, parents getting divorced, etc. To counteract this feeling of helplessness, being able to dive completely into one's self can create a hiding place where a person can concentrate on a different kind of pain.

Once the root cause and the why for Cindy's beliefs about her body have been established, it's time to start practicing an alternate way of thinking that will counter these negative and false thought patterns. She may have a discussion with loved ones about how she doesn't value others based on their weights. Why should she hold herself up to this standard? What does her weight have to do with being a good or strong or valuable person? There is a difference between being thin and being healthy, and thin people are not necessarily healthy. Giving Cindy hard facts about the state of her health may help her wake up a bit in terms of where she is physically — stressing the importance of fat to the body's functions, to muscles health, to bone health, to mental health, etc. These facts will help her start to form a new, better informed picture of what it means to be healthy and beautiful.

Substance Abuse

Substance abuse has many forms and manifestations and will prove to be one of the most difficult forms of addiction to conquer. We've talked about the mind forming habits of thought based on false belief systems, but the forms of addiction involving substances denote a whole different level of addiction which causes specific chemical processes to happen in the brain. Once these forms of addiction take root, the result is that the body will fight incredibly hard to keep this addiction in place, causing withdrawal symptoms should the sufferer decide to make a change. This is why most people who become addicted to substances end up on a seemingly endless cycle of cessation and withdrawal, followed by falling back into their old habits. An approach to recovery that involves CBT is going to necessitate a much more rigorous, constant schedule of intervention as the addict's body begins immediately to rebel against getting clean. Rehab centers are set up as a way to provide constant care as well as constant watch over the behaviors of those who are admitted. Typical daily therapy may include sessions focused on helping the patient come to terms with the origins of his/her addiction, how it got started, whether or not it was encouraged, etc. A much more difficult but necessary topic will be assessing and coming to terms with how this person's addiction has affected his/her relationships, especially loved ones.

Loved ones are often the catalyst which drives a person with a substance abuse problem to admit themselves to full-time care in an attempt to be free of their addiction. When these attempts fail, loved ones often see this as a sign that their loved one who is suffering is choosing the substance above those he/she loves, but this is not necessarily a correct perspective. Addiction is a serious bodily affliction, and unless the patient's loved ones have also experienced substance abuse addiction, it is going to be very difficult to reach an understanding between the patient and his/her family and friends. Instead of fueling hurt feelings, it will be necessary for everyone involved to commit to starting fresh and focusing on the sufferer and his/her situation. CBT will probably force the addict to think of painful memories and circumstances, but it is going to be very important that the addict stop running and face what is going on. Running away in thought is going to encourage running away in the form of feeding substance abuse addiction.

Whatever the motivation for making a change may be, the sufferer is going to need to work through, step-by-step, what has brought them to the place they are. Working through and letting go of the emotions that have accompanied past trauma or abuse will be necessary to set the mind free of obsessive thinking and cultivate habits of consciousness so that the sufferer stays on top of his/her feelings and compulsions. CBT will offer tools and strategies to help combat the thought processes that will inevitably creep into the patient's life in order to convince him/her to use again. The tools must be in place, and the patient must believe in him/herself to be able to find the strength to think of how much more important other things and people are in life than substance abuse. Successfully overcoming a compulsion once is not nearly enough to start celebrating yet, but it is essential to acknowledge that victory to enforce a belief that the patient can repeat the success over and over again until bad habits are replaced.

Low Mood, Self-Esteem, and Toxic Relationships

Just as with all other human emotions, low mood is something that will come and go within a healthy human being's lifetime. But a persistent low mood accompanied by detrimental thought patterns will signal that intervention is necessary to change this downward spiral. Depending on the severity of the mood symptoms, there are many tool and strategies available for everyone to develop as a way to combat these negative emotions. Taking time to sit down and write down a list of things you are grateful for maybe all it takes to turn a low mood around into a positive one. Low self-esteem can often be reversed with some consistent encouragement and support from others whom the individual respects, loves, or admires.

Chronic self-esteem issues are usually propelled

forward by an experience or series of experiences which make the person feel as though they are not good enough in some way. This could be the product of bullying, failing a test, not making the cheer squad…the list goes on and on. Low self-esteem can lead to forming those false belief systems we've already talked about. Those belief systems can be anything from, I'm not cool because she won't be friends with me, I'm worthless because I didn't make first chair in jazz band, I'm never going anywhere because I can't get that promotion, etc. These negative habits of thoughts will only serve to keep a person in place when they desire desperately to move forward. CBT applied in these situations will focus on prying lose those negative belief systems. It is important for the patient to understand that by cultivating those negative beliefs, they are giving other things and people power over their lives when it is unnecessary to do so. A person must dig deep to understand their personal motivations for where they place their value, then reconstruct their belief systems and self-value based on concrete truths about themselves and their worlds. They must be armed with the tools to mentally counter those thought patterns and replace them with truths and other, positive thought patterns to support and empower the individual.

Finally, the effects of a toxic relationship can also be addressed through consistent cognitive behavioral therapy in order to break a person free from toxic dependence and chronic low self-esteem issues brought about by that relationship. This can be complicated by the presence of the person who was cultivating that toxic relationship, and it may be necessary to help the sufferer get physical distance from this person in order to heal. Living in fear of this person is going to halt the potential progress he/she could be making through therapy. Unfortunately, this is often complicated by the presence of children, making it impossible to expel a toxic person from the sufferer's life completely. However, it is not impossible to come to terms with the situation and reform the sufferer's self-esteem and positive outlook through self-empowerment, awareness, focusing on life's priorities, that he/she deserves happiness, etc. Strategies will vary based on each situation, and though it seems insurmountable at first, CBT has been proven to bring people to places they never thought possible following the most traumatic experiences imaginable.

Cognitive Approaches

Cognitive behavioral therapy is an approach that focuses on human cognitive function. Instead of trying to force changes in behavior, practitioners realize that behaviors stem from a process of thought which has developed its own system over time as influenced by a myriad of factors in the realms of nature and nurture.

To get a better understanding of why CBT approaches work the way they do, let's look at a few examples of individuals who have constructed a cognitive paradigm contributing to an anxiety disorder.

Josh is a college sophomore who is struggling with trying to decide which classes to take and what kind of career he wants to make for himself. He also tends to steer clear of any class which he knows will require him to speak in a presentation format in front of the class. He suffers from debilitating social anxiety and hates it when people look at him.

Where did this anxiety come from, and how did it develop? Let's examine Josh's life from childhood. Keep in mind that the development of mental illness and mood disorders is as varied as the people who are afflicted by them. We are only looking at an example.

Josh grew up as an only child and spent a lot of time by himself. His parents doted on him in the form of buying him presents and letting him play sports and get involved in activities, but they also never spent a lot of really personal time with him having conversations or talking about difficult subjects. Josh was a very quiet person and usually only had one or two friends to hang out with at any given time during his childhood. He performed well in school but suffered socially and occasionally annoyed the few school bullies who targeted the more awkward kids.

As he grew older, the bullying got worse as he became interested in art classes and was made fun of by the boys in his class. He became nervous in 8th grade during a class presentation because the boys who bullied him kept giggling and laughing at him, and he felt embarrassed. By the time Josh got to high school, he had become quite socially withdrawn, though he maintained close friendships with a few friends who also considered themselves outcasts. He continued to do well in school and felt a little more empowered as he got good grades and started thinking about his future. This positivity fell by the wayside, however, when he became interested in a girl. He was determined to impress her and ask her out, so he bought some new clothes and practiced what to say in front of a mirror. She was a lot more popular than Josh, but he thought he could see that she was a cool person who wouldn't see things that way.

One day after school, Josh works up the nerve to talk to her as she is hanging out with a friend. The interaction is more awkward than Josh had intended, and though she was very nice to him, she declined to go on a date with him.

The experienced should have ended there and was not altogether unpleasant. She wasn't mean to him at all. But the boys in his class and the bullies who had followed him outside tormented him every day for a week, making fun of him for thinking he could go on a date with a pretty girl.

Josh let these things get to him, and he decided that he probably would not ever find a girl who could like him because of his oddities and social awkwardness. The thought made him sad, and he wanted to cry but felt he couldn't do so unless he was hidden in his room where no one could see. Crying only solidified that he wasn't really a "man" and more of a child, in his mind.

Like many other young men entering college, he went through the motions and got into a school quite easily. It wasn't a fancy school, but it was a good distance away from his hometown, and this is something he wanted. He wanted to try and escape his past and have a fresh start. Maybe he could become a whole new person.

Josh continued to do well academically, but whenever he saw or met other guys who reminded him of the bullies he'd had to deal with in high school, his insecurities and shyness would intensify and he would make himself small, as if he felt automatically subservient to them. The feelings would arise during even brief presentations, so he avoided classes that had a class presentation requirement on the syllabus. Sometimes his anxiety became so bad, he would start to experience an odd sense of panic where his chest would tighten, his heartbeat would start racing, and his breathing became abnormally hurried. It would last just a few seconds, but it was alarming enough for him to go to an on-campus doctor for an exam. She told him that he was experiencing panic attacks.

Fast forward to sophomore year, and we've gotten up to speed on Josh and his life experiences so far. So, what can we deduce about Josh's mindset, and how might he be experiencing dysfunctional cognitive thinking?

As mentioned earlier, the factors that go into how a person develops a disorder like this are varied, and no two people's experiences are going to be exactly alike. There are some interesting facets to Josh's life which may shed some light on how his social anxiety developed, and these things would probably be brought to light as part of a cognitive behavioral therapy plan for treatment.

First of all, Josh has to consider that his genetics have played a part in his personality. We didn't go into his parents' personalities, but we do know that he was fairly shy as a child and was never particularly outgoing. This is a personality trait, and it may have been exacerbated by the fact that he was an only child and spent a lot of time alone, playing by himself. A child who is outgoing may overcome this circumstance and make lots of friends to hang out with because of a magnetic and fun personality. Though Josh was a nice person and may have been fun to hang out with, he did not have the assertive personality to go out and find friends.

Josh's lack of social interaction would have culminated in some social awkwardness, and this would have been blatantly contrasted with others he saw around him who did not seem to suffer from any social awkwardness. He would have seen the popular people going around and talking with lots of people, always welcomed warmly. As human beings, especially at high school age, we tend to compare ourselves with others around us. Men learn very early as a product of social learning and instinct that it is important to do your best to climb the ranks of society. Those who hold higher positions in society are usually the best protected. Those at the bottom of the social ladder are not considered as essential, so for whatever personal motivation, young men will strive to look good, perform well, and be popular. Those who fail in any of these regards tend to let this reflect poorly on themselves in their own minds. Unfortunately, this often translates to others taking notice and categorizing these individuals as obviously less capable and valuable. Once this identity is established, it would have been very difficult for Josh to have climbed out of his category without a complete personality change, which of course doesn't usually happen. He was relegated to the unpopular table for the remainder of his high school career, finding solace only in his few fellow "loser" friends.

Experiencing this kind of delineation in high school is something most people carry with them for a long time, maybe even the rest of their lives. Some people live with resentment or frustration. Others may find success and are able to shed those feelings of not being capable like the popular kids. Josh natural shyness and lack of experience around people led to a degree of awkwardness which persisted through his years in school. The embarrassment that accompanied these perceived shortcomings were magnified by the cruel reactions of his classmates. For this reason, over time, Josh develops an automatic thought (which we will define more in depth in the next pages) which is connected to his paradigm he's developed which defines himself as a person of low social stature and capability. His instincts in social situations are hindered by these belief systems telling him that he is going to fail, even if he is quite capable of successful social interaction.

In college, there are many different personalities and many kids with whom Josh might connect and have relationships with, but his experiences in high school may cause an automatic translation of new people in his mind which equates them to the limited personalities and categories of people from his high school experience. He is not the only socially awkward person on campus, but his mind has isolated itself in this definition and perceives all others to most likely be more capable and therefore just "better." This thought process will keep him from recognizing others who may be receptive to his unique personality because he's already made up his mind about how people are going to react to him.

His panic attacks arise as his obsessive thoughts feed his fear of speaking in front of people and being looked at by other people. He's been over the experience of failure and inadequacy so many times in his head that it's almost like he fails before he's even tried. He recalls the feelings of embarrassment and hurt from his past and projects these experiences onto his current situation, even if no one is actually trying to make fun of him or is laughing at him.

When Josh sees a psychologist about his panic

attacks, he is diagnosed with social anxiety, and it is suggested that he give therapy a try.

Now that we understand Josh's history and struggles with anxiety, let's take a deeper look at how a therapist or psychologist might define what's going on inside Josh's mind.

Automatic Thoughts

CBT works in a way that focuses on peeling back layers of thought, progressing to the deepest layers possible. What exists in the deepest layers of cognition, subconsciousness, belief systems, personality traits, morality, etc., influences what exists at the surface of cognition. Automatic thoughts are the immediate thoughts that exist on the surface of cognition. These thoughts feel like free will assessments but are fundamentally influenced by what exists in those deeper layers of self and the mind. An example of an automatic thought would be the snap judgment a person makes when he/she sees someone whose skin is a different color from his/hers. Depending on that person's history, experiences, personality, and belief systems, this automatic thought could be any one of many automatic thoughts. If the automatic thought is fear or intimidation, it might indicate that this person has not spent much time around people of that particular race and the ignorance in his mind has been filled with fearful speculation about that race's characteristics. This is a form of racism stemming from ignorance and the mind's eagerness to fill in missing information with what he/she has heard from others in his community, family or friend circle. A person who is brought up with family members constantly making racist comments and without having experienced any contact with someone of that race will inevitably have preconceived notions when that person does finally meet someone of that race.

We can extend this concept of automatic thoughts to

an endless list of underlying belief systems and thought processes. What is the automatic thought when you hear a news story about guns? When you see a small child without shoes? When you see a cop walking around the block? When you hear jazz music? All of these automatic thoughts have a deeper connection, and sometimes this connection is toxic and eats away at a person from the inside.

Josh's automatic thought when he sees someone casually looking at him in a classroom may be one of many different thoughts connected with his deeper belief that anyone who looks at him is going to make fun of him. He may automatically think that this person is noticing something about him which is odd, making Josh feel self-conscious and the compulsion to remove himself from the room to get away from the anxious feeling rising in his chest. In reality, there is no evidence that this person is trying to make fun of Josh, but the experience has been so solidified in Josh's brain that this seems like the only possibility to him.

Intermediate Beliefs

We might imagine ourselves walking backward from the automatic thoughts toward a deeper layer of cognition called intermediate beliefs. Intermediate beliefs are the attitudes or rules which a person adheres to as his/her personal guide as he/she navigates the world. These attitudes are founded on the person's core belief systems and may be positive, negative, hurtful, inaccurate, hateful, loving, etc. In Josh's case, we might pin down several intermediate beliefs which form his automatic thoughts as he engages with the world around him.

As Josh sees a pretty, socially capable young woman, his intermediate belief may be that he is not allowed to approach her because she is on a higher level than himself. His automatic thought process will originate from this belief and cause something like an instant reaction of "nope, off limits."

In the example above where Josh begins to feel uneasy when someone looks at him in a classroom, his intermediate belief may be that because someone is looking at him, it means he looks funny and should leave. This belief feels concrete in his mind as he's fallen back on this belief so often as to make it a firm habit. He doesn't have to think through the situation to arrive at this conclusion. This is where the work of CBT would meet some challenges.

Other intermediate beliefs which hold a strong influence over Josh's emotions will involve beliefs that work to hold his low self-esteem in place, causing his anxiety around others. The intermediate belief causes something of a domino effect whenever Josh is met with a social situation. His ability to work through his experience rationally is completely hindered by the belief systems that keep reinforcing his inadequacy.

Schemas and Core Beliefs

Walking back further into the deeper areas of cognition, we find schemas and core beliefs. These beliefs are going to be deep-rooted and often stem from childhood experiences and the belief systems that were either handed down and taught by parents or others in a position of authority or developed as a result of childhood experiences. Let's explore some different possibilities for these developments.

Many parents are determined to hand down their religious beliefs, and in an effort to do this, they start bringing the child to religious gathering and classes as early as possible. The child is immediately surrounded by a community of people who believe similarly, and thus, the child is brought up in a way that constantly reinforces this religious belief system. Many people grow up with this belief system firmly instilled in their minds and continue to follow that religious belief for their whole lives. Others may be introduced to alternative forms of religious belief systems and decide to follow those, or simply decide that religion is not for them at all. Though we are inclined, as human beings, to follow patterns and fill in missing information with information gathered from others or our similar experiences, we are also keenly curious and exploratory animals. Many kids in their teenage years find alternative pathways which go in opposite directions from their parents' pathways. This would be the result of a genuine conviction or a simple act of rebellion and an effort to move away from the parents' control. Whatever the case, these core beliefs are formed as the individual makes decisions about his/her reality and the rules that govern it. Emotions play a role in the formulation of these core beliefs as childhood experiences, and teenage experiences are often associated with strong emotional feelings. Many people attest to a special feeling they get when they are in church or another religious setting, and they attribute this feeling with a religious presence, solidifying their core belief system and accepting all of the communally accepted dogma associated with such beliefs. It's the phenomena that once you've accepted one small core part of an organization's belief system, it feels necessary and only rational to accept all of the beliefs which are connected to that core. For example, when a person is brought up in a Catholic church and accepts that God is real and active in his/her life, it falls naturally in place, most of the time, that this person accepts all of the rituals and adjacent beliefs that are associated with Catholicism.

Similarly, a person may move away from the church and subsequently reflect and all associated beliefs and rituals just because they are connected with the religious entity that this person has rejected. They make the decision that religion is fundamentally and rationally flawed. Therefore, all associated morality and adherence to ethics are meaningless. Again, these constructs may be the product of simple investigation and rational decision-making, or it may be a rebellion and rejection based on negatively charged emotional experiences connected with religion or an authority's attempted enforcement of such a belief system.

Let's look at Josh's situation and try to determine some core beliefs from which his anxiety has developed. Based on his poor experiences with other people from a young age, Josh may hold the core belief that shy people are not as good as outgoing people. This core belief was probably formed and reinforced by the fact that Josh constantly saw outgoing people surrounded by friends, while he struggled to find social connections at all throughout his childhood and teenage years. Another core belief may stem from the longevity of this particular experience, leading to the belief that there is nothing he can do about his status. There is nothing he can do to change who he is and his worth, and he is doomed to be socially unacceptable for the rest of his life. This core belief would feed into the intermediate belief in a particular experience with a woman that says, she is pretty and sociable, therefore off limits. These core beliefs would be gradually approached through CBT sessions until Josh has fully brought them to the light and assessed their existence and the reasons for their existence. He will also recognize the deep emotional associations he's cultivated through constantly throwing himself under the bus in any and all challenging social situations. Even the mere thought of speaking to people has become overwhelming because of the weight it conjures that is filled with sadness and defeatism. The next step for Josh will be to start questioning the rationality of his core beliefs.

Logical Questions and Evidence

One of the fundamental trademarks of cognitive behavioral therapy is the practice of challenging cognitive processes and demanding a logical explanation. This process helps show the sufferer that many of the belief systems in place in his/her mind actually stem from irrational interpretations of emotional experiences.

In Josh's case, he might be asked why he believes he is socially unacceptable and what the evidence is for this. He may consider himself a failure because he's never had lots of friends. Why has he not historically made lots of friends? He may say that it's because he is socially awkward. The counselor might then mention the few close friends which he's connected with because they are similar in personality. Does he consider them lesser people because they are awkward? This might be a difficult question and hopefully will start the ball rolling as far as tearing down false belief systems. When did he decide that being socially successful meant having lots of friends? Have you ever met or heard of someone who is lonely despite being surrounded by lots of people? Many people have lots of friends but not a lot of close people they feel they can really trust and relate to. Josh has met people and made good friends, isn't this a success? When has he ever taken the time to feel gratitude for these people in his life?

Josh's feelings of inadequacy are often triggered as he associates current social experiences with the experiences he had in the past with bullies in school. He may be asked to relive his experience in the classroom where he perceived that someone who was looking at him was really making fun of him in his mind. What evidence does Josh have to support this belief? Or does it simply resemble a past painful experience, and his mind is trying to protect him from that experience?

The question and evidence approach may be used to address any belief system which Josh has managed to bring to the surface. Those who have caused consistent negative emotions are going to be prime targets for this type of investigation. The reality what we want Josh to reach is that past experiences do not dictate present ones. The projection of a negative reality he once knew is an illusion covering up what is actually present and going on in his life now. As the logic begins to break down his systems of though, Josh may start to realize how fragile and emotionally grounded his belief systems are and, hopefully, be able to prepare himself for the challenge of reworking his thought processes to begin forming a new, rational and positive paradigm for his life.

Evaluation of Thinking

Once Josh figures out how erroneous and hurtful his patterns of thought actually are, it is time for Josh to really evaluate what is going on as he makes immediate and negative associations and interpretations in his daily life. A starting point may be to challenge himself to fully engage with the experience the next time he feels the familiar creeping up of anxiety in a social situation. There will probably be a lot of opportunities on campus to examine his natural reactions more clearly.

When he enters a classroom, he may feel the familiar gut feeling that everyone is watching him and secretly making fun of him for some reasons. Maybe it's his clothes, the way he walks, the way he's styled his hair, etc. In this situation, Josh may try to engage with this feeling and ask himself, why do I think this is happening? His mind will struggle to give him a rational explanation for these feelings, and Josh will soon realize that this experience is based almost entirely on emotional connections from past negative experiences. Nothing in the past has any bearing on what's happening to him now, and there is indeed zero evidence for his belief that anyone in this classroom is paying attention to him. In fact, he may conduct some small experiments on his own to try and gauge how much people are actually paying attention to him. If he looks around the room, he will probably notice that most of the people in the room have their eyes on a screen of some sort, or perhaps they are making small talk with those who are already seated in the area. The key realization here for Josh is that no one is, in fact, making fun of him, or indeed paying much attention to him at all.

As Josh moves through his day, the more he can make these kinds of observations, the more he will begin to retrain his mind to think differently and consequently, feel differently. As he challenges these preconceived notions about his reality and what he's supposed to feel, those connections will be broken, and new neural pathways will begin to take their place.

This is not a quick nor easy process, and it will take a lot of time and investment of energy on the part of Josh. But hopefully, as with anyone who decides to start CBT, the slow progress will be a welcome change from feeling forever stuck in a seemingly inescapable negative cycle of thought, emotion, and behavior.

Behavioral Assessments

Now that we have a bit more information and understanding regarding the emotional and cognitive goings on involved with a mood disorder like social anxiety, let's take a look at how behavior is assessed and addressed through cognitive behavioral therapy treatment.

We will use a new example for this chapter, this time looking at some key aspects of depression behaviors.

Sarah is a young woman in her mid-20s who has just been diagnosed with depression. She is beginning cognitive behavioral therapy to address something called cognitive distortions as well as irrational beliefs.

Depression is a potentially devastating mental illness which affects a lot more people than most people think. Depression and mental illness, in general, are associated with a high level of stigma from the general public who have no experience with mental illness. Depression, in particular, can be looked at like an indication of a weak person who simply has low confidence and self-esteem. But for those who have firsthand experience with depression and their loved ones, they know that depression is a very serious thing that requires consistent, rigorous treatment in order for the sufferer to see improvement in symptoms.

We will look at an example of depression to address behavioral assessment and cognitive distortions because there are a lot of thought processes which depressives tend to have in common.

Emotion and Behavior

Human behavior is often intimately connected to emotional experience and can tell us a great deal about a person's emotional status. For example, have you ever seen someone who just exudes a bad attitude? He may have very poor posture, his eyes downcast, brows furrowed, perhaps he makes very little eye contact with anyone he approaches, etc. As humans, we pick up on patterns of behavior and tend to assign them to an emotion or an attitude if they stand out in some particular way. It is usually pretty obvious when someone is incredibly happy and full of joy because their behavior is going to reflect that. Similar, someone who is going through depression will usually display signs that betray their emotional state, even if they are trying very hard to hide it. Of course, this is easier to read for someone who is familiar with depression and the person in particular.

But depression, because there is so much stigma associated with it, is often something people are ashamed of, and they may go to great lengths to try and hide what they are feeling from others. This can result in even further isolation and falling even deeper into the depression.

Even more dangerous is the tendency for a person's behavior to encourage or perpetuate those feelings that are symptoms of the depression. This pattern of emotion and behavior becomes a vicious cycle, making it very difficult to break habits.

Let's say Sarah tends to hold herself with poor posture and a general scowling look on her face. This behavior often causes a reaction from people, which is not positive. People may look at her and mirror her facial expression, which Sarah then interprets as that person thinking ill of her, which she then internalizes as truth, and the cycle thus continues to gain support.

Many people develop behavioral habits in response to depression, which are physically unhealthy and quite destructive. Drugs and alcohol as forms of self-medication can lead to incredibly serious health problems and lifelong struggles against addiction, which only further perpetuates a cycle of depression. The longer a person with depression goes without support or treatment, the more they become convinced that they are in a helpless and hopeless situation.

When we become convinced of a belief, human beings tend to focus in on only those patterns which perpetuate and support that belief system, especially if the alternative of realizing you are wrong about something presents a possibly unbearably painful experience. This is part of the habitual aspect of emotion and behavior. A person who is depressed and convinced of her hopeless situation will likely fail to see glimmers of hope or opportunities for treatment or support because they are only focusing on that which supports their belief systems. We see this everywhere with all kinds of belief systems, not just with mental illness. People like to feel confident in what they know and don't like to be proven wrong. We all like to think that we have all the facts we need to make an informed opinion, but we are often wrong, especially about really important things that are accompanied by a strong emotional component.

Irrational Beliefs and Cognitive Distortions

Psychologists have identified and defined many different kinds of cognitive distortions, which lead to irrational beliefs. Cognitive distortions are defined simply as persistent errors in thinking. We will discuss a few of the most common ones and relate them to how Sarah may be experiencing them in her life with depression.

The first is "all or nothing" thinking. Oftentimes

individuals with depression will have convinced themselves that the world works in opposing extremes. They are either good wives or horrible wives. They are either good people or bad people, they are either really good at their jobs or really terrible, etc. There is no gradient or standard or middle of the road in this type of thinking. This is why this type of thinking over time can lead to feelings of major downturns and upturns in life. Everything is either all good or completely bad. Further, a person with depression will have already developed a habit of focusing on only the bad, so this type of thinking will work to augment a bad situation into something unbearable bad.

Another common distortion of people who are depressed is the habit of thinking in a way that completely discounts the positive in any given situation.

Let's say Sarah is recently married, and she and her husband are thinking about starting a family. They hesitated because of Sarah's depression, and she begins to imagine that she is a terrible wife because she is not ready to have children. This belief may stem from the intermediate belief that all women who are married and in their 20s should have kids. The fact that she does not mean that she is a failed woman in some way. Even if her husband consistently explains to her that all he cares about is her wellbeing and that he loves her no matter what, she will continue to interpret his words in a way that is consistent with her false belief systems. He is only saying these things to make her feel better, but secretly he wishes he was married to someone better, etc. The facts that they have had a great relationship with little fighting, a nice home, and are financially stable do not even enter her mind as she only focuses on the fact that she has not given her husband children yet. Granted, this is a pretty old-fashioned example, but there are plenty of people who still hold similar belief patterns based on their parents' and previous generations' lifestyles.

Another quite emotionally powerful cognitive

distortion is an insistence on labeling. Sarah is quick to label herself as a failed woman and a failed wife because she is not ready to have kids.

There is an adjacent phenomenon which women like Sarah may be suffering from in the midst of a depression. Oftentimes, the originating belief which triggers symptoms of depression may metastasize into a collection of beliefs which support the same cognitive distortion. For example, Sarah believes that she is not a good wife because she should have kids at this point in her marriage already. She may also begin to feel that she is also not a good wife because she doesn't have a perfect body, a beautiful face, or because she doesn't always take care of their home to make the house looks immaculate. She may be taking time off from work to try and treat her depression and also feels that she is a worthless wife because she can't bring in money and help her husband pay the bills. All of these beliefs support the underlying intermediate belief that she is a bad wife.

Overgeneralization is another common distortion in which, similar to a black and white thinking pattern, the person believes that a truth that applies to one component of a group applies to the entire group. Let's say that Sarah also struggles with feelings of jealousy in her relationship. She tends to internalize these feelings and beat herself up, thinking that feeling jealousy also makes her a bad wife because "no man wants a jealous wife." She may believe that her husband desires other more attractive women and believes that is a behavior that applies to all men. This kind of thinking is destructive because it feeds a belief system that every single person in this group is this way. Therefore, a reality without jealousy and betrayal in a relationship is nonexistent. Not only is she projecting a behavior onto her husband (desiring other women), but she is also applying this behavior to all men, and therefore, she will never be in a happy, committed relationship. This further perpetuates the looming black hole of hopelessness which characterizes depression; the conviction that everything is awful and that there is also no hope that it will ever change.

Exposure and Systematic Desensitization

One of the ways cognitive behavioral treatment addresses and treats various mood disorders and mental illness is through a process of exposure and systematic desensitization. At the heart of the problems underlying each disorder is an adamant adherence of the mind to a pattern of habitual thought cycles and belief systems. It is very important for the sufferer to be able to analyze his/her thought patterns in order to address how they are affecting the quality of life. Behaviorally, it may also be necessary to practice physically adjusting habits which are holding the patient back from living. Let's revisit anxiety disorders to outline an example.

Acute anxiety tends to adamantly discourage a person from engaging in behaviors or putting themselves in situations where there are triggers for that anxiety. You will remember Josh and his refusal to sign up for any classes in which he will be required to stand up in front of the class and speak due to social anxiety. How might exposure and desensitization help him overcome this fear?

He's already come along this far in working through how his thought processes are flawed and based on an irrational paradigm. He's even gone so far as to challenge his anxiety when he feels himself coming up against a trigger. A next step, which will be even more challenging, would be to purposely put himself in a situation that will cause anxiety in order to work his way through the emotion and come out the other side. The purpose of this exercise will be to demonstrate to himself that his fear is not just irrational and illusory but also very temporary. He could do this in many different ways. Perhaps he could challenge himself to have a conversation with that cute girl he thought was out of his league. His task might simply be to talk with her about the class for one to two minutes, then excuse himself. He doesn't have to ask her out or do anything crazy, just a simple casual conversation. What might he experience during this experiment?

Well, he will have probably guessed that his anxiety will be at a 10 on a scale of 1 to 10 at the very beginning. He might experience a near panic attack as he walks up to her, anticipating her reaction and dreading the worst outcome possible. If he's practiced his thought interruptions, he will dispel this thought and replace it with the fact that he has no evidence for such fears and that what he is doing is completely acceptable.

When he opens his mouth to speak the first few words, the words may come out a little jumbled, and his breath may not be steady, or he may be taking deep breaths. Perhaps beforehand, he will have practiced how to smile and maintain eye contact while he focuses on the fact that he is simply having a casual conversation with a girl. Several behavioral tricks he may have learned would include holding himself up in good posture with his shoulder back and his head up. Research shows that simply adjusting one's posture in public can boost a person's confidence to a large degree. Making eye contact and smiling are positive signals which tell another person that you are being open and are friendly.

The key to exposure and desensitization is to sit in the uncomfortable emotion for as long as it takes to feel it start to dissipate. Josh will feel the highest level of anxiety at the beginning of his interaction with the girl, but as the conversation continues, he will notice that his anxiety starts to drop as he becomes more comfortable. This is a key breaking point that Josh will need to repeat in order to address his anxiety fully. The more he challenges this fear around people; the more his brain will re-learn that there is actually not that much to be afraid of.

In Sarah's case, there may be a need for significant cognitive work before trying anything resembling Josh's experiments with anxiety. But if there are behaviors associated with Sarah's depression, which are avoidant and detrimental to her quality of life, then exposure will be another tool for her to use to rise above this negative influence.

One of the hardest and most baffling tendencies of a depressed person in a romantic relationship is the development of the belief that they are unworthy of this person's love. Sarah may feel like such a failure that accepting support and love from her husband is extremely difficult. In conjunction with talk therapy, she may be tasked with challenging herself to be more accepting of her husband's love and support as she challenges the notion that she is undeserving or unworthy.

A specific task may look something like this. When she comes home from work or her husband returns home from work, there may usually be a period of time when they used to hang out and talk, or Sarah would receive a hug and kiss from her husband. She hasn't been letting him do this for several weeks, but now she will try to accept this from her husband. Just as with Josh in his exposure task, there will probably be a lot of anxiety surrounding this action, simply because Sarah has become accustomed to the thought pattern that she doesn't deserve this attention. When she does finally let herself receive a hug, she will probably experience a wave of emotion that she did not expect. This would be an important first step toward letting the vital support of her husband re-enter her life as she battles her depression cycles.

Exposure and desensitization is a strategy used for many different kinds of phobias, and it all works in a similar way, no matter the fear triggers. A person who is terrified of spiders may begin an exposure behavioral therapy by just looking at a picture of a spider for a few minutes. The patient might keep a journal about how her anxiety and fear feels as she accomplishes the exposure task. Her fear at the outset might be a near panic, but as the seconds pass, she will notice the fear start to lower as her mind starts to realize and accept that she is not, in fact, in any danger. Eventually, the fear will rest at an all-time low, even though she is still looking at the picture. This would be an incredibly positive first step.

A similar process may be used for someone who is afraid to leave his house. Many people develop agoraphobia, which is characterized by a fear of putting yourself in situations which may cause embarrassment or a panic attack. In the most extreme cases, this fear becomes so looming that even the thought of walking out your front door is terrifying, and so a person may become trapped in his own home until he is helped through treatment.

Exposure in this situation may first entail therapy, which helps him identify the core of his irrational belief systems. It will be very important that he realizes that this sense of danger is not based in fact in order to start adjusting his thought patterns. When he is ready, his first step may be something as simple as looking out the window and gauging how this makes him feel. What does he think about as he looks out across the front yard and into the street? What is he afraid would happen if he walked across his front lawn?

The key to these exposure tasks is a gradual escalation of challenges, in addition to acknowledging and sitting in the fear until it dissipates. The hopeful outcome of such a therapy technique is that the patient will gradually teach his/her mind that the things which he/she was afraid of doing do not actually deserve such an intense anxiety reaction. The process will, of course, vary from person to person and may last for a longer or shorter amount of time depending on the severity of the symptoms and the willingness of the patient to be an active participant in his/her recovery. Sometimes it takes time for a person to work up to a point where they feel they are ready. As mentioned earlier, taking physical steps to address a phobia is only going to be effective if the person has worked through the cognitive distortions first. A person must understand where such thoughts are coming from in order to make a good, effective argument that these beliefs are irrational. This is important for long-lasting benefits.

Functional Analysis

We discussed earlier about how sufferers of mental illness, like depression, may turn to self-medication as a coping mechanism for their experiences. Functional analysis in CBT comes into play in order to assess the role of substance in a sufferer's life in order to help him/her come to terms with why this is a part of his/her life. The counselor may ask a series of questions which are designed to really target all of the circumstances surrounding the start of substance abuse; emotional state, mental state, what was going on in the person's life, what were possible triggers, how was the idea introduced into the person's mind in the first place, what was the rationalization for using, etc.

This will probably be a difficult conversation to have, especially if there is still some element of denial going on. At the foundation of substance use, the user simply gets addicted to having a way to run away from the uncomfortable fears, anxiety, depression, etc. Substance use essentially feels like a complete erasure of everything that plagues the user's mind. Most people who turn to substance use do so as a near last resort when everything seems hopeless, and there does not seem to be anywhere else to turn. There may be a social component in which substance use is associated with camaraderie with others who are also suffering or trying to deal with similar problems. The longer a person indulges in the behavior, the more they will be able to strengthen whatever story they've told themselves to justify their behavior. Cognitive behavioral therapy may help to unbury the truth and lift the veil that substance use introduces in the user's life. When the user realizes that this way of life is not solving any of his/her core problems, then they may be ready to start a rigorous therapy treatment to get on the path to recovery.

As mentioned before, most of the time, it will take several attempts before a user successfully frees him/herself from the clutches of substance abuse. Addiction is a powerful thing and should not be trivialized or underestimated. There is nothing more demoralizing to a user than someone making comments about how they should be stronger or better or that they can't get clean because they don't actually value or love other people in their life, etc. A strong support system is almost always vital for a person to see themselves at the end of a recovery treatment plan. At the same time that they are battling physical addiction, they are also battling cognitive distortions and flawed thought patterns telling them to think and act and feel in a way that supports their addiction to substance and self-destruction through thought. Belief in one's self is incredibly hard to cultivate when you don't have anyone else in your life who also believes in you and your ability to progress out of that dark place.

The origin of a person's substance use may stem from something traumatic or from a simple desire to get rid of uncomfortable emotions. What a substance user usually discovers too late is that the promise of erasing those feelings are false and the ensuing addiction often involves even more painful emotional responses and struggles. The user will start to see how their behavior is affecting those around them who care for them but may feel helpless to get themselves out of the situation.

A rehabilitation center is set up for the user to have 24/7 supervision and care while he/she goes through a painful and challenging process of trying to break the addiction. The process will incorporate therapy to address cognitive issues while also offering support for physical discomfort and withdrawal symptoms.

Coping Skills

The light at the end of the tunnel when it comes to

cognitive behavioral therapy is the progression to learning coping skills and strategies for countering negative thought patterns in real time as the person lives his/her life. The individual has explored to an extensive degree all of the problematic thought processes which have contributed to a mental disorder or illness and is now ready to learn how to move forward. Many times, it is not possible to eradicate a mental illness altogether, but the goal of CBT is to arm the sufferer with knowledge and tools so that the illness no longer keeps them stuck in the same place, unable to move forward or accomplish anything they want to do in life.

One of these coping skills is the creation of counter thoughts which the patient will use each time as a trigger is experienced. The goal is that through consistent practice and use of this countering thought, the old habit of going immediately to fear or sadness or anger is stopped in its tracks and replaced by a more productive, positive reactionary thought process. Let's look at an example using our old friend Josh.

Josh's main trigger comes in the form of other people and his fear of feeling embarrassed or doing something incorrectly. Whenever he enters a room or is tasked with speaking to someone he doesn't know, he will have created some counter thoughts to combat the anxiety that may threaten to rise in his body. Instead of thinking of inevitable failure, he will instead recall the last time he rose to a challenge and successfully got through the experience, like when he approached that girl in class and had a brief conversation without freaking out. This thought is a positive one that encourages confidence and dispels feelings of inadequacy and fear. He will use this weapon, as well as any other useful counter thoughts, to retrain his mind to think a different way in situations that used to cause him great distress.

This practice assumes a level of mindfulness. Mindfulness and awareness are some of the core tools a person can utilize in an effort to combat negative emotion because they demand a person always be using their rational, actively thinking brains instead of deferring to emotions. It is a skill that must be practiced and honed consistently in order for the practitioner to experience the full range and capacity for benefit. We will cover additional tools and tips for combatting flawed thought pattern in chapter 6, but first, we will try to reach a greater understanding of anxiety and depression and how these construct false realities in a sufferer's mind over time. Understanding depression and anxiety is essential for understanding the ways to combat them and why they are effective.

Depression and Anxiety

This book focuses on cognitive behavioral therapy and its application to treating depression and anxiety. We've looked at many of the cognitive dysfunctions that characterize mood disorders and mental illness as well as the various approaches CBT utilizes to address irrational thoughts and restructure the way a patient thinks in relationship to the world.

In this chapter, we will go a little more in depth into the worlds of depression and anxiety. We often hear about these two disorders in conjunction with each other, or as "comorbid" conditions. Oftentimes one fuels or triggers the other to appear in various situations. We will first look at how anxiety may form and take over one's thought processes and how this can intensify over time.

When we examined Josh and his anxiety as an example, we looked at social anxiety in particular. There is a broader form of anxiety called generalized anxiety disorder, which is characterized by a constant feeling of worry, helplessness and fear, which affects day-to-day function. It is very difficult to pin down exactly how something like this develops in the brain. Many scientists and psychologists heavily attribute childhood experience and upbringing as well as a genetic component which makes individuals more likely to develop anxiety disorders. People who do not suffer from such a disorder find it very difficult to understand why a person would torture themselves like this day after day. What exactly does a person with generalized anxiety disorder experience?

Let's see if we can find a better understanding by

living a day in the life of Joe, a 50-year-old man with a generalized anxiety disorder.

An individual with generalized anxiety disorder, like Joe, experiences a kind of overwhelming sense of impending disaster that blankets everything else in life. Where a neurotypical person may wake up, brush their teeth, eat breakfast, then start thinking about their to-do list for the day, Joe wakes up and immediately feels a weight in his chest and mind about what lies before him. His mind begins working overtime as he struggles to get out of bed and go about a normal morning routine. In his mind, his thoughts are racing from one event to another, perhaps remembering an embarrassing event that took place last week, recalling the frustration of being late to work two days ago, dreading a meeting that is scheduled for the end of this week, and worrying about the traffic he will have to face if he doesn't get out of the house in exactly 30 minutes. He slowly gets out of bed, wishing he could just stay and never leave the house again. He forces himself up and to the bathroom to take a shower and brush his teeth. He goes to the kitchen and gets out some cereal he bought for himself at the store yesterday, but the knots in his stomach keep him from really wanting to eat. His brain tells him that he would rather stop at a fast food place and get something really sugary or starchy, and this may become a habit if he starts to associate this experience with a sense of relief and momentary distraction.

On a side note, eating unhealthy, tasty foods is often a form of coping mechanism for people with anxiety disorders because it temporarily distracts them from the chaos in their minds, giving them something enjoyable to focus on. It could be thought of as another form of destructive self-medication, and those who are diagnosed with anxiety disorders also often present with weight problems. Joe, on his way to work, is desperately seeking something to ease the worry and discomfort in his mind. The idea of stopping to buy something tasty on the way presents itself as a kind of wall to slow the eventual, inevitable arrival to his workplace. This would be a very easy thing to make a habit every single day if he decides it is worth it just for those few minutes of distraction.

So Joe stops at McDonald's and gets a breakfast combo with a coffee. He listens to the news on the radio as he wraps his mind around the obligations in front of him. When he eventually gets to work a few minutes later than he'd planned because of his breakfast stop, he now has to get out of the car and walk into the building. Just as Josh struggled with the idea of people looking at him and judging him or making fun of him, Joe dreads walking in to the building each day because he knows he will be expected to perform typical social interactions with his coworkers and pretend to be perfectly comfortably even though he is nearly panicking inside.

Joe walks through the large double doors of his office building and sees the receptionist. She waves and smiles, and he does the same with his best effort at a smile. As he walks into the area where his cubicle sits, he passes several of his coworkers who stop to say good morning and offer more smiles. Joe does his best to respond to each of these interactions as he makes his way to his desk. Someone surprises him as he comes up from behind and taps him on the shoulder. Joe jumps, nearly spilling the hot coffee in his hands, and turns to see who is trying to get his attention. It's a guy named Sam, whom Joe finds loud and obnoxious. He wants to shoe Joe something on his phone that he finds hilarious, and Joe does his best to pretend to be interested. Finally, Joe makes it to his desk and sits down.

Joe has a lot of work to do, and then suddenly remembers that one of the higher-ups is visiting to take a look at the office today. His heart jumps into his throat as he imagines this guy coming up to him and asking him a bunch of questions he won't know how to answer. The scenario plays over and over in his mind, each time he gives a more stupid answer and feels the entire office staring at him as he fails miserably. The thought distracts him from his work, and his pace is much slower than usual. By the time lunch comes around, he has not even finished half of the work he had planned on finishing. The weight of this reality piles on top of the anxiety he already feels, and he again hopes to escape through leaving the office and going to get a big slice of gooey pizza from the pizza place next door.

As Joe starts to walk out of the office, a few of his coworkers invite him to have lunch with them, but he declines, making an excuse that he has a bunch of phone calls to make. When he gets outside, he regrets not being able just to go and talk and relax with his coworkers. He does not have a lot of friends to hang out with, and it would be nice to have some support in his office environment. Unfortunately, in his mind, Joe believes he would stumble through conversations and look like an idiot because his mind would not be able to focus and relax. He walks by himself to the pizza place and gets the biggest, unhealthiest slice of pizza he sees in front of him and sits down to eat it. The big boss will be in the office when he goes back, and he briefly contemplates jumping on a bus and running away, never to be seen again.

Instead, he finishes his pizza and gets up to return to the office with a few minutes to spare on his lunch break. When he gets back to his desk, he sees the bosses gathering across the hall and discussing something as one of them gestures into the room where he is sitting. He hopes desperately that they won't walk by him and try to ask him questions. He formulates a plan in his mind that if they get too close to him, he will take the long back to the bathroom and simply stay there for a good 20 minutes until hopefully everyone has left the area. He pats himself on the back for finding a solution to this problem, then gets back to his workload. Nearby, he hears a couple of his female coworkers having a conversation. One of them is a woman named Sandra, and he has worked with her for almost four years now. He has developed an attraction to her but considers her way out of his league. He listens as another person approaches the conversation. It is Scott, one of the new hires, who is in his thirties and very sociable. This is enough to completely shut down any hope in Joe's mind, even though Sandra is much closer to Joe's age than to Scott's. Joe has managed to have a few conversations with her over the years, but they'd never had a really personal conversation. The very idea of trying to open up to a woman is too terrifying to contemplate.

Joe constantly compares himself to other professionals around his age in his office building and always finds himself coming up short in nearly every category. He is balding, not in the best shape, and even though he's worked there for years, he has only received one raise. His house is not that nice, he doesn't have any nice collections or art or really any hobbies to speak of. He considers himself a pretty boring person because the only thing he has energy for in the evening is watching TV until he nearly falls asleep and drags himself back to the bedroom. He uses so much energy just to get through a day without having panic attacks that his life has become really nothing more than worry, fear and a struggle to move forward and pretend to function normally like everyone else around him. In this kind of life, there is no room for hobbies or relationships. He finds it difficult enough just to stay alive, and the pressure has started to really weigh on him.

As the bosses enter the room where Joe is working, he gets up from his desk and goes to the bathroom. He feels ridiculous sitting in a bathroom stall for 20 minutes, but it's not nearly as intense a feeling as the fear of having to talk to his bosses. When he returns, the bosses are gone, and he lets out a sigh of relief. He looks at the clock and realizes he only has a couple more hours to get through his day's workload and gets to work. He is able to focus on his work a little bit better than before because he has the end of the day to look forward to. He has almost made through another day filled with anxiety, and soon he will be able to drive home and release all of the tension he's built up by completely melting into the couch and not moving for probably a good four hours.

He feels somewhat satisfied with his accomplishments as the clock hits 5 o'clock and he's gotten through 90% of his workload. He decides he will come in a little early the next day in order to finish and get a head start on tomorrow's tasks. In the middle of his relief at having reached the end of the day, he suddenly remembers that he will have to participate in a meeting in two days, and his stomach drops to the floor. All of the relief and looking forward to being able to relax dissipates almost instantly, and he knows that now he won't be able to think of anything else for the next 48 hours. The only thing he can do is try and distract himself with some greasy food and some TV. He drives home listening to the same radio station as he did on his morning commute, stops to buy some takeout on the way, then sits in front of his TV once he arrives. This is Joe's daily life cycle, and over the years, it has gotten worse and worse until he is basically a prisoner of his thoughts and cognitive distortions.

Selective abstraction is another form of cognitive distortion in which a small detail is taken out of context and focused on while all of the surrounding information is ignored. Joe has integrated this practice into a habitual routine which colors his reality and steers his mind toward only the stressful details which fuel his anxiety. His day has been full of cognitive distortions.

Joe begins each day by giving way too much weight to the events in his past and in his future. The idea of going to a meeting in a few days feels almost the same as if he was expected to participate in a gladiator contest to the death that afternoon. Why is this so blown out of proportion? The seed of anxiety about any given situation begins when we start to focus on what could happen, and this possibility is a worst-case scenario. We try to prepare ourselves for the worst by concentrating on this possibility, but soon, it is all we can focus on. This cycle is self-perpetuating, and if we let it, this thought pattern can turn into a full-blown habit in which every situation is looked at through a lens of cataclysmic probability. Instead of looking at the meeting as a typical meeting where, like all past meetings, there will be some dissemination of information followed by a brief presentation and then a questions and answer session, suddenly we become convinced that we are going to be called on to speak unexpectedly, or that there will be bad news, etc. This fear and worry is a powerful emotion and takes the place of rational thinking in this situation. Joe's anxiety disorder has made this type of thinking and cognitive distortion a part of his life on a nearly constant level.

Let's say that one day, Joe starts to realize the toll that his anxiety disorder is taking and decides to speak with a therapist who recommends a process of cognitive behavioral therapy. We can reference a lot of the methods that Josh, in our previous example, was introduced to here. Joe will need to get at the bottom of his anxious thought process in order to address the real problems underlying them. What is the basis for his low self-confidence and constant worry? What evidence is there for him to go off of that tells him terrible things are going to happen? What is the basis for believing that he will embarrass himself through normal every-day work-related tasks and conversations? Was he an awkward child, or was there an embarrassing event that his mind recalls any time he interacts with other people? These associations will have to be worked through in order to break the automatic association with his present situations, as they are only holding him back from living them.

The Progression to Depression

Let's look at how depression may develop from Joe's situation and experience with generalized anxiety. Isolation and loneliness are often cited as key triggers for serious, chronic depressive states, and Joe's anxiety has worked to isolate him in every way essentially. He isolates himself at work for fear of being awkward or doing or saying something embarrassing, and he's isolated himself outside of work, refusing to interact with others and form friendships because his mind is overwhelmed with the anxiety and desperately needs a break after work. He can't even fathom the amount of energy he would need to engage in a social event after work because he is barely making it through the work day before his body and mind give way to complete exhaustion at home. This doesn't make him happy, but it is necessitated by his cognitive distortions and constant anxiety. In fact, he recognizes that he is very unhappy, and perhaps he doesn't know what to do about it. Therapy is not a matter of telling someone else your problems, then having them solve them for you. It takes effort and consistency on the part of the patient. But let's say Joe begins to notice new symptoms which prompt him to seek help.

Joe's constant isolation begins to feel like a weight

on his chest that feels like something even heavier than the fear or typical anxiety he is used to waking up with. He finds that on some days, he barely has the strength and motivation to stand up in the morning, almost like he has the flu or some other kind of chronic illness. He is lethargic almost to the point where he cannot work, but the fear of losing his job gets him out of bed and on his way to the office, even though each day is a massive struggle. He finds that it is becoming much harder to pretend to be normal each day as his smiles are completely faked and feels zero interest in everyone around him, even the attractive woman named Sandra whom he has always felt an attraction for. On his way home from work one day, he becomes tearful suddenly and begins to cry openly in his car. He is instantly worried that other people around him in their cars will see him, but it isn't enough to stop him from crying.

When he gets home, he crashes on his couch and realizes that he feels deeply depressed and unable even to get himself to make dinner. He decides it is time to talk to a therapist.

At this point, Joe is afflicted with both a chronic anxiety disorder that he's dealt with for years and a burgeoning depression. When his therapist diagnoses him officially with depression, she offers to walk him through a process of cognitive behavioral therapy and explains the basics for how this would get started. He agrees.

When describing a depressive state, Beck's cognitive triad is often cited and used as an explanation for a person's belief system in the depths of depression. They are: negative views about the world, negative views of the future, and negative views about oneself.

Joe's anxiety causes him to think a great deal about the past, present and future, but all of these realities are engaged with through selective abstraction and what's called magnifying and minimization, where the positive aspects of his life are minimized and the negative aspects are magnified. For example, in a typical workday, Joe will acknowledge that he does not have friends to hang out with during lunch, that he will never get the girl he wants, and that he is behind at work. The positive aspects of his life may be that he has a job in the first place, lots of available work, and an open opportunity for him to accept invitations to have lunch with coworkers or start a conversation with Sandra. This distortion keeps Joe in the dark about opportunities and possibilities which may improve his quality of life. He must address this before he can begin to make changes and adjust the way he thinks and views the world.

Let's look deeper into Joe's thought process using Beck's cognitive triad. First of all, Joe exudes a negative view of the world. This is reflected in his attitude about nearly every extraneous interaction he experiences outside of his home. The traffic in the morning is not cars filled with other people; they are simply an inconvenience. His coworkers simply torture him with politeness and annoying conversations, and his bosses are simply out to embarrass him or catch him in a mistake. He doesn't particularly enjoy his job, but he finds it absolutely necessary to suffer through, and the idea that he could find another job is something he doesn't seem to acknowledge as a possibility. So basically, the world is a place he must trudge through day in and day out with very little enjoyment outside of his TV and his unhealthy food.

Second, Joe has a negative view of the future. Joes does not see his situation as something that can change in any way. He dreads future events that he has no control over, like his staff meeting, and has already decided before it's even happened that something terrible or fear-inducing will happen. He can't imagine a scenario in which the meeting is pleasant or laid back or not a scene of pure torture. He also has resigned himself to the following week, and the meeting that comes after that week, and the one after that, and so on. His future is bleak because he has already decided what it will look like. When we decide we know that our futures are bleak, we completely shut down our ability to see possibility or opportunity, or really anything other than the bleak reality we've created in our minds. This is another essential point Joe will need to address in his CBT sessions. There is a possibility, there is an opportunity for change, and no one should be living in misery the way he is.

The third side of the triad involves a negative view of oneself. This is a pretty ubiquitous viewpoint across sufferers of anxiety as a common trigger for worry and even depression is the idea that one is "just not good enough" in some way. For Joe, he has never felt confident enough to ask for a raise at his job, even though he's been there long enough to do so. He does not believe that he is better than his station. In fact, most days, he is overwhelmed with the workload he already has. He also considers himself well past his prime to have any hope of finding a meaningful relationship, much less with the girl of his dreams, Sandra. He does not consider his health to be a concern he should invest in because he considers himself a hopeless cause. He may not have thought this in so many words, but the fact that he lets himself gorge on unhealthy food whenever he wants a break from the anxiety tells us that he really doesn't value himself or his body. Many patients who have come in for therapy for depression and anxiety actually state that they think they were subconsciously trying to kill themselves through unhealthy eating, gaining absurd amounts of weight with no control whatsoever. We can see Joe possibly heading down this road.

All sides of the triad must be addressed before Joe is ready to take some steps forward, but he must find a personal motivation to improve his life; a therapist can provide support and encouragement, but it is up to the patient to put in the work to make real changes. This is why no one can be forced into effective therapy. You can't drag your loved one suffering from depression into a therapist's office and expect magic to happen within one session.

At the very beginning, it is very important not to overwhelm a person suffering from anxiety and/or depression with an extensive plan of therapy. Perhaps the first step is a simple conversation with someone who cares. People in this situation often blind themselves to the fact that there are people around them who care and want to help. It is important that these individuals present themselves and offer their time, even if it's just to sit in silence with the sufferer. Remember, one of the most common triggers for depression, and even suicide is chronic isolation.

Once you've gained the individual's trust, then it may be appropriate to present the idea of therapy. Support and encouragement are so vital in this scenario, as well as giving the sufferer someone who will listen to what they have to say. Simply talking through issues and destructive thought patterns can be a big step forward in understanding where a person has gone wrong in their thinking.

Once an individual is ready to take on the challenge, the next step is a formalized treatment plan, and the time it takes to complete such a treatment plan will vary widely according to each patient's situation and needs.

Set Measurable Goals

Part of taking action in a treatment plan that involves cognitive behavioral therapy will be a schedule of small steps toward goals that can be measured and evaluated. It will be important that the patient see that he/she is making progress, and not just running around in circles. The chaos inside the mind of someone suffering from depression and anxiety will hinder their ability to see the way forward and appreciate how far they come. Each time the patient reaches a milestone, it will be important to acknowledge this as a success before setting the next one. The milestones should be things that are within the person's scope of possibility, and they should not be trying to do too much at once because this will only set the person up for failure. Set small, measurable goals that can be accomplished and reflected upon as the patient moves forward.

In the next chapter, we will go over several tips to help see this progress to the end of a successful recovery.

Hacks and Tips

Overcoming debilitating conditions like depression and anxiety is never an easy thing to do, but there are things that each person can try as they move through their journeys, learning from themselves through therapy, medication, or lifestyle changes. In this chapter, we will introduce several strategies and changes that may help a person who is going through cognitive behavioral therapy themselves, or else looking for alternative ways to deal with the chaos and stress that comes from a chronic mood disorder or mental illness.

Identify and Break Negative Thought Cycles

This is arguably the most important as well as difficult step a person will take. Negative thought cycles are at the core of what perpetuate the disorder and trap a person in the same place so that they do not move forward. CBT is an excellent tool for this progression out of entrapment, but there are things an individual can do on her own to take steps in the right direction on her own.

Becoming mindful and practicing mindfulness meditation may be one way to retrain your brain each time you are in a moment where the familiar negative emotions begin to creep up on you. The key to mindfulness is staying aware of your thoughts as they occur instead of surrendering to them and the emotions they trigger. Allow yourself to question what is happening when a familiar negative thought comes into your mind. Ask yourself, why am I having this thought? What use is it? How is it affecting me? What evidence do I have to support the validity of this thought? Am I just addicted to the emotional responses?

This last may be a key factor in a person's persistent emotional struggle. Emotions can be addictive, just like any other more familiar forms and sources of addiction. When we decide that life is horrible, we tend to create circumstances and events in our lives, which support the idea that life is horrible. Have you ever woken up in a bad mood and then experienced an unending stream of bad luck and mishaps throughout that day? Most of us have, at some point in our lives. This is the concept of the "law of attraction" at work. You may be familiar with this concept from the wildly popular film called "The Secret" which was released several years ago. The Secret film was all about the law of attraction and the idea that whatever you want in life, you can attract by simply focusing on your goal, consistently visualizing yourself having reached that goal, and being ready to take advantage of the opportunities as they come to you. Now, it is easy for some to take this to a very pseudo-science, new age level, but at the core of the concept is a nugget of gold that holds true in terms of the human psyche.

When we are focused on only the bad happening to us, then we fail to see the positive or see opportunities to change our realities. Oftentimes in this situation, we simply fail to realize that we are capable of making positive changes, creating a trap for ourselves in which we experience the cycles of negative emotions over and over again. This is not the way anyone wants to live, and there is certainly a way out of this rut if you are willing to question and counter those thought processes holding you captive.

A mindfulness meditation practice may help you to weed out just what is motivating the negative thought cycles and feeding your depression and anxiety. Just like you would do in a therapy session, you can practice engaging with your own thoughts in the privacy and comfort of your own home. Start by accessing some of the most debilitating and painful thoughts your mind throws at you throughout the course of a normal day. Is there one central thought that remains the theme of your moods, or do you go through a large pool of thoughts that may or may not be related to the same core belief? I may help to write down notes as you home in on your personal reality and the driving thought patterns behind it. Engage with how this thought makes you feel. Is it painful? Does it make you sad? Feel hopeless? Useless? Do you experience negative self-talk? What is the voice telling you? How often do you let the voice influence how you are feeling or how you function? Immerse yourself in what you are feeling. Don't try to run away just yet, especially if that is your normal habit. You have to engage and work through these feelings and thoughts if you are ever going to dispel them and take back control of your life. Sit in the emotion and feel the effects of these thoughts. Stay in the moment, write down what you are going through.

Now your challenge is to ask yourself the same kinds

of questions you may be asked during a CBT therapy session. At the core of this investigation is trying to make you realize that your belief systems and thought patterns are flawed in some way. Whether you are minimizing and magnifying, overgeneralizing, labeling, etc., those thoughts which are causing you pain have been given an irrational degree of power over you through your thought habits. Once you wrap your mind around this truth, you can begin to restructure how you think about each concept.

Pick one of these habitual thoughts and take some time to challenge it. Write down or think about alternative realities or truths which would counter the one you are used to. Ask yourself if it is possible that you are worrying or fearing something that doesn't deserve so much fear and worry. Are you making a big deal out of something instead of dealing with it? Is what you are afraid of actual danger or just a possibility that you can't get out of your head? If you've figured out that the causes of your emotional turmoil are inflated and not based in reality, then it is time to start replacing this through pattern with a new one that is based in reality and your ability to guide your own life.

However, we should also talk about the possibility that your fears, anxieties or worries are a result of real and present danger in your life. Are you involved in a toxic relationship right now? Do you feel trapped? If there are people or circumstances in your life which are hurting you, manipulating you, or making you miserable in some other way, then no amount of therapy is going to cure that for you. You will need to address this danger in a safe way with support behind you. If you don't have family or support from friends, then go to the police or a community support group. Do whatever you need to do to start moving away from this negative influence. Sometimes it is a matter of breaking ties for a while with friends who are encouraging self-destructive behavior. Maybe you feel stuck in a terrible job that makes you miserable. Don't resign yourself to years and years of misery. You can find another way and a better, more positive way to live your life. Don't be afraid to ask for help, and don't let other people take control of your life.

Mindfulness meditation can help bring you to a state of calm so that you can begin thinking clearly about your situation and what you need to do to start creating a better life for yourself. Start by choosing a quiet, comfortable spot in your home or living space. Try to choose a time and place that is not likely to be interrupted by other people or outside noises, etc., as much as is possible. Now, find a comfortable position to sit and relax your muscles as much as you can. Begin to breathe deeply, in and out. Breathe slowly and deeply. Count to 5 at the top of your breath while holding it, then let the breath out slowly, counting to 5 again. Repeat this a few more times until you start to feel your body relax, and your mind starts to slow down a bit. Don't be surprised if it is very difficult to reach a place of relaxation when you are first starting. Your mind is going to want to run all over the place. But with consistent practice, setting aside some time each day to meditate, you will start to associate this time with calm and quiet, both outside and within yourself.

Now, think about the place you want to be mentally and/or physically. You are familiar at this point with your struggles and the thought cycles you have to deal with, but right now take some time to visualize what it would be like if you did not have to worry so much or feel anxious or depressed. What would you look like? How would you feel? What would you want to do? Are there others with you enjoying life right along with you? Try to visualize this reality with as much detail as possible. Don't let go what this feels like, looks like, sounds like, etc. Many people who practice meditation suggest using a mantra to help reinforce a certain truth for yourself or a goal. Start with something basic but strong, such as "I am enough, I am strong." The idea is to say these words either to yourself or out loud. Concentrate as each word leaves your mouth and really be present in what you are trying to say. What does it mean to be enough? How are you strong? Think of times in your past when you did display the idea that you are enough or a kind of strength. What was the situation? How did it make you feel? What challenges did you conquer? Can you remember what the scene looked like? Etc. Start to conjure this scene or memory in your head if you can remember clearly enough. If you can't remember all the details, it's ok to make some up to fill out the scene. The important thing you are trying to conjure is that feeling of strength and accomplishment that probably stayed with you for some time after accomplishing your task. Did you share this feeling with others? Who was with you sharing this moment? Perhaps those individuals could work as a support network for you now, if they are still around.

As you conclude your meditation session, move back to your breathing pattern, and remember to end on a positive note by smiling to yourself. As mentioned before, it has been proven that altering your posture and your facial expressions will adjust your mood almost instantaneously. So give it a try! Smile and soon you will start to think of things that are worth smiling about in your life. Concentrate on those positive forces and practice feeling gratitude. Gratitude and cultivating thankfulness for anything and everything positive in your life is a great way to begin countering the incessant thought patterns that only emphasize what is wrong or hurtful in your life. Gratitude meditation is a very effective way to begin forming a positive mindfulness habit alongside mindfulness.

Journaling

Writing and journaling can be a powerful form of therapy, no matter what you are dealing with or how you are trying to overcome those forces. Writing about your struggles and specific episodes will help you come to terms with yourself and your thought patterns, as well as how destructive such patterns can be. Sit down and set aside some time to write about some of the big things you can't stop thinking about when you are feeling anxious and/or depressed. Perhaps it goes outside these barriers into a certain phobia, insomnia, or persistent panic attacks Flesh out on paper as clearly as possible what you are going through. Treat the paper like a therapist and spill all the details of your experience that you can manage. Don't hold back out of fear of embarrassment or shame or whatever other emotions are holding you back. This is all part of the process. You must get to know yourself and the core of your struggles.

As you move through a CBT treatment schedule, keeping a journal will provide an immediate source of encouragement and motivation as you look back on your progress over time. There is really no going wrong when it comes to journaling. If you are concerned about other people in your life finding and reading your writing, you may choose to keep the journal with someone you trust instead of in your own home, or else use a password-protected word processor online. Some people will prefer to write by hand in cursive while others will prefer typing. Choose whatever is most comfortable for you.

A journal is also a great place to start having a conversation with yourself. Ask yourself questions, be your own therapist. Outline your personal goals and spend time thinking of what steps you could take to get to those goals. Set your own pace and try not to compare your progress with that of anyone else. We are all unique with our own unique problems. Though they may be similar in some respects to other people's problems, we are still unique human beings who are going to need to deal with each of our problems in a way that is right for each individual. Just because one strategy worked very well for someone else with depression, doesn't mean it's going to work in the exact same way for you. In fact, this is really quite unlikely. We all have our own roads to travel down.

Get Out of Your Comfort Zone

This one probably sounds a little scary, but that's the point. You may recall from previous chapters that we discussed a treatment approach called exposure and desensitization. You don't have to wait for a therapist's schedule or a specific treatment plan to take the first important steps yourself.

At the core of your harmful and irrational belief systems, thought patterns and emotional reactions is a habit. Habit is at the foundation of nearly everything that is giving you trouble in your day-to-day life, so naturally, in order to change the trajectory of your life, you will need to practice breaking old harmful habits and creating new ones. To break an old habit, you are going to have to travel outside your comfort zone.

Let's take our old example of someone who has agoraphobia. He may be at a point where he doesn't even like to leave the house for fear of what may happen. He understands that this is an irrational fear, and he is ready to challenge that fear by taking baby steps away from this habitual way of thinking.

His first small step maybe just to go outside and sit on his porch. That's it. It may seem like quite a meaningless step to someone who isn't suffering from agoraphobia, but for him, it's going to mean a very big step into the great unknown. He may choose to go out in the evening when there are likely fewer people outside to see him, or he may choose to challenge himself by dressing himself in a nice outfit and stepping outside his door in broad daylight when he is sure to catch the eye of a neighbor somewhere in his vicinity. It's all about taking baby steps and challenging himself as much as he can handle. He may decide to stay out there for a few minutes or an hour. If he thinks he can handle an hour, perhaps sitting and reading a newspaper or a magazine, then he will have accomplished a very big task, and he should be proud of himself for doing this.

Someone who is socially anxious may challenge herself to finally say yes to that coworker's dinner invitation after work. The idea of meeting up with these people, though she knows they are nice, is one of the big things triggering her anxiety. She may ask herself questions like, "why am I anxious about hanging out with them?" "Why do I think I'll mess up?" "Have I ever done something unforgivable at work around these people?" Then, she may encourage herself by thinking about how, even after so many refusals, she still gets an invitation, and what's more, she seemed quite excited that she finally said yes. That means these people are actually looking forward to her company. Keeping these positive thoughts in her mind anytime her anxiety tries to get her to focus on that bad possibilities is very important in making sure she follows through with the challenge.

It can be very, very easy for someone suffering from depression and/or anxiety to begin immediately making excuses for not following through with challenges like these. A person with anxiety may feel a surge of hope and self-confidence and say yes to a social invitation, only to let their minds convince them to cancel at the last moment. This happens because they've succumbed to the same old anxious thoughts which convince them they won't have a good time, that it's not worth it, that they don't really want him there, etc. You have to arm yourself with positive, self-assuring thoughts beforehand so that you are ready when the time approaches and the anxiety starts to ramp up. Your depression may try to tell you that you are not worth other people's time, that you are only going to bring people down, etc. These are not the thoughts that are going to get you through to the other side. Even if you don't think you will enjoy yourself, try making it a challenge that is about just getting yourself to go out the door and be somewhere other than your living room. Once this challenge is passed, you will see how good it feels just to know that you've conquered something that is extremely difficult for you. You walked out that door. You greeted your friend. You walked into a busy bar. You had a drink or two. You joked and had conversations, then you left the bar and came home. A night like this for a socially anxious person can feel like hitting a home run.

Problem Solving and Skills; Education then Implementation

One of the tools taught during a cognitive behavioral training treatment plan is learning to problem solve in the difficult moments when the patient's negative thinking is trying desperately to take over. The person suffering from anxiety or depression will need to be able to identify and differentiate fact from fiction in terms of their reality and what their minds are trying to tell them. Something like this may seem very simple to someone on the outside, but it can actually be quite confusing as the sufferer's mind translates the world around him much differently from most.

Learning as much about your particular condition as

possible is a great way to prepare you for understanding and dealing with the way your mind interprets the world as someone with anxiety or depression. Whatever treatment plan you decide to pursue, it will be an important component to know when what you are thinking and feeling is based in reality or a paradigm you've constructed in your mind. The closer you can come to identifying and differentiating in these situations every time, the closer you will be to creating a new way of life that gives your active, conscious, positive mind the controls.

In addition, consider seeking a group of people who meet weekly for sessions as a way to hold yourself accountable to a regular routine of talk therapy and getting support. It is very difficult to face a challenge like this alone and having others around you with whom you can relate can give you a really big boost in your motivation and positivity regarding your therapy or treatment plan. It is very helpful to look around you and discover that you are not the only one going through something like depression or chronic anxiety. Let others into your life and give yourself permission to feel vulnerable. There is a degree of trust that is demanded in an environment like group therapy or a support group, but the benefits will come back to you tenfold. Give it a try, and you may find new lifelong friends who will be happy to help you or walk alongside you on your journey to **a better mindset.**

Conclusion

Thank you for making it through to the end of Brain Rewire, let's hope it was informative and able to provide you with all of the tools you need to achieve your goals whatever they may be.

We've covered a great deal of information in this book, and hopefully, you are not overwhelmed but instead inspired to move forward, whether you are educating yourself for the sake of helping a friend, or simply exploring new possible avenues for your own treatment plans. The more you learn about cognitive behavior therapy and the research to support its powerful results, I feel confident that you will discover relevant and significant ways in which the implementation of this treatment plan can help you or your loved ones conquer the devastating effects of anxiety, depression and associated symptoms and conditions. There is really no end to the benefits that a regular cognitive behavioral therapy plan can offer. The tools that can be found during the course of treatment will remain as strong and powerful throughout the course of one's like as they were at the outset.

In chapter 1, you learned the basics of cognitive behavioral therapy and who it is used to treat. The application of CBT extends far and wide and goes much further than anxiety and depression. CBT has been used to treat war veterans suffering from PTSD as well as many other mental diseases like schizophrenia and severe phobias. You learned about the basic principles of CBT and the steps involved in a standard process for treatment. Many of the principles and action steps in CBT are ideas that can be implemented in personal practice through meditation or journaling.

We went in depth into several of the most common mood disorders and mental illness afflicting the modern world today. Anxiety and depression are much more widespread than most people realize, due mostly to the still prominent stigma surrounding mental illness. Many people suffering from such conditions choose to suffer through months or years of symptoms before finally giving in to the fact that they need help. Some people are embarrassed even to talk about something like that going on in their lives.

The cognitive approaches to treating such conditions follow a fairly methodical series of treatment plans which aim to engage with several facts of the human mind and how it is functionally flawed in the grips of the conditions like anxiety and depression. In chapter 3, we outlined some of the common terms used in psychology to illustrate a person's core beliefs, intermediate beliefs, and automatic thought processes.

We discussed how these could develop from early experiences as well as how they can be influenced by a genetic component in families where there is a history of mental illness. We learned how a typical course of CBT would actively focus on challenging flawed thought processes through evaluation of thinking and asking questions to challenge the logic of certain thought patterns and digging for evidence or lack of evidence in each situation.

Behavioral assessments looked at how emotion and behavior work together to cope in destructive ways through substance abuse in many extreme cases where individuals are in so much pain that they look for anywhere to run away. Common self-medication techniques like drugs and alcohol offer temporary relief, but the individual pays dearly for this over the long term with dire health effects and usually much deeper sources of pain and shame. Also, in this chapter, we discussed how habits might start to be redirected through strategies like desensitization and exposure therapies.

You learned a lot about how anxiety and depression seep into a human psyche through examples and demonstrations of these processes in action. We've also discussed some of the terminology and definitions of key dysfunctions in the mind involved with anxiety and depression, including cognitive distortions and their many forms.

Finally, we hope you found a few of the tips listed in chapter 6 to be useful and interesting. We encourage you to try as many of these techniques as possible if you feel they may offer you some advantage in your journey toward recovery, or in the journeys of your loved ones.

Finally, if you found this book useful in any way, a review on Amazon is always appreciated!

155

Manipulation and Persuasion by NLP

Essential Guide to Neuro-Linguistic Programming and the Dark Psychology Secrets to Social Influence and Manipulation Protection

Introduction

Congratulations on downloading *Manipulation and Persuasion by NLP* and thank you for doing so.

In the following chapters, there is so much to learn about how to use persuasive speech and body language to get what you want from others. You're in for a fast ride through the dark side of psychology. We'll take a look at the history of persuasive communication and the important psychologists who made it all happen. Learn techniques for reading the body language of others in order to draw insights that no one else can see. Learn to implement effective and versatile tactics to gain adoration, get you the job, get you the partner, and even get you the car you know you deserve.

Hold on tight as you cruise through huge value like how to protect yourself from dark manipulation, coercion, and predators, how to skip the logic and get right to the imagination, how to know if you're talking to a looker, a listener, or a toucher—even how to lie. This book is packed with tricks for how to customize your mind and program outcomes you want from yourself and from others. You will walk away from this book, stealthier, wealthier, and dripping with confidence.

But you'll also learn places to go for sharpening your skills and how to use records and measurement to improve over time. This is essential for the eager professional who wants to learn systematically, practice often, and gain territory fast.

There are plenty of books on this subject on the market, thanks again for choosing this one! Every effort was made to ensure it is full of as much useful information as possible, please enjoy!

Dark Side of Psychology

Dark psychology surrounds us. It is inside of all of us, lurking, shrouded in a dark blanket of mystery and fear. It's in the bus driver, the daycare provider, the dog walker. It's in the tone taken with you, the posture of the stranger beside you, the favor someone asks for help with, and the tone of a teacher.

At first glance, you may not see it at all. You may not even think twice about the person who held the door for you. Dark psychology is often overlooked or misinterpreted. And therein lies its power. People are unaware of the dark psychology tactics that surround them every day.

Dark psychology is still real psychology but it deals with the behaviors of the individual, which may be construed as darker behaviors. Specifically, these behaviors are used to manipulate their surroundings and those who play a part in it.

When we talk about these qualities in the media, they are often associated with predators taking advantage of others to get what they want.

But the theory is these qualities exist within us all. Manipulation and persuasion may be a way for some to get what they want from others but it could also be the coping mechanisms used to survive a violent or abusive situation. Persuasion and manipulation can exist with some degree between employees and employers. Even pet owners and their pets have a degree of this in their relationship. Ivan Pavlov and his dogs? It's conditioning others to agree to the outcome you want and the work it takes to get there.

To gain a stronger understanding of what is meant by the phrase "dark psychology", it's smart to take a step back and refresh ourselves on a bit of Psychology 101. Here, we are reminded that there are typically six classical schools of thought in the study and application of psychology.

Structuralism

Functionalism

Behaviorism

Cognitive Psychology

Gestalt Psychology

Psychoanalysis

Psychoanalysis is the one everyone is most familiar with, by way of study or movies and media leaking into your perception, whether true or only perceived truths.

We are most familiar with psychoanalysis because we know who Sigmund Freud is.

While the school of psychoanalysis did initially play a significant role in its development, Individual Psychology really lands somewhere between Cognitive and Gestalt schools of thought. It's Alfred Adler who puts it there. It is from Adler's seeds that sprouts the study we know today as dark psychology.

Meet Alfred Adler

At the start of the 20th century, Dr. Alfred Adler makes one of the most influential contributions to the study of psychology to this day: Individual Psychology.

In his famous break from Freudian psychoanalysis, Adler suggested that the individual was not able to be divisible into id, ego, and superego the way Freud had suggested. Instead, Adler proposed that the individual is an indivisible entity affected greatly by his surroundings and those within it, particularly beginning in young age.

Adler himself was born in Austria in 1870 as the second of seven children to a merchant and his wife. Suffering his own childhood traumas, Adler lay in bed beside his own brother as his brother died. Later, Adler met his own ills; contracting rickets, which kept him from walking until about age four or five. Nevertheless, Adler grew up with a generally normal lifestyle where he was an average student and shared a healthy competition with his older brother. Adler was said to have recalled the exact moment he decided to become a physician. He had developed pneumonia and a doctor had come to assess him. The doctor told Adler's father there was no hope for his son and it was at this point that Adler decided he wanted to be a better physician than this man.

Adler attended the University of Vienna and then later explored subjects such as psychology, sociology, and philosophy. Adler began his professional study in ophthalmology but changed directions and took up general practice. During WWI, Adler served the Austro-

Hungarian Army as a doctor an eventually settled as a neurologist and psychiatrist. After the war, the doctor was able to continue work on his studies and published a set of theories and principles based on his popular and unique lectures from 1912-1914. During his early practice, Dr. Adler had established an office in a much less affluent area of Vienna and as a result, often worked with downtrodden workers and circus performers. It is said that these experiences and observations are largely responsible for the development of Adler's theories.

It was not until the start of the 20th century that the dynamics, the motives, and the tactics of persuasion and manipulation began to get the rigorous observation and development of theory and therapy.

Adler, along with Rudolf Reitler and Wilhelm Stekel joined Freud, by Freud's invitation, met each Wednesday evening for the benefit of sharing theory and experience. Out of these meetings grew the psychoanalytic movement. Though Freud and Adler shared a mutual respect for one another, Adler did break away from Freud's famous psychoanalytic practice and later even refused to associate with the label. Adler enjoyed success in carving his own path and introducing the new psychology—individual psychology. Adler's contributions to psychology, particularly from 1912 - 1914 is considered to be extremely influential and a foundation stone to much of the counseling and psychiatric care strategies today.

The Adlerian school of thought focuses on understanding the individual as a sum of his environment and exposure and personality and cannot be divided for observation or study. Much of Adler's work also involved the theory of an inferiority/superiority complex, suggesting that it was the individual's greatest need to attain superiority and as a result of this need, the individual's thoughts and behaviors utilize manipulative means to acquire that. These actions are often driven by a person's belief that they are inferior in some way or many ways.

The Adlerian school on Individual Psychology has played a significant role in the Humanistic Psychology studies of leaders like Carl Rogers, Maslow, and Viktor Frankl. Dark psychology is the study of the darker human behaviors, yes, but it is also because these personalities are regarded as undesirable and get less attention and study than the positive psychology personality traits.

Professor Del Paulhus (who you will learn about in a moment) insists it's the dark personality traits that are more fascinating and revealing when it comes to human behavior. It's on the dark side that Paulhus contributes significantly to psychology. It is in the study of the personality types and traits of an individual driven to manipulate that we find ourselves in the midst of dark psychology.

From Individual to Dark

With the understanding of individual psychology—the idea that the individual is the sum of personality, surroundings, and subjective experience—we are able to uncover the study of traits, behaviors, and actions associated with preying upon and taking advantage of others. This is the dark side of psychology.

Called dark and separated from psychology as a whole, this study is a bit of manipulation in itself. The traits and behaviors associated with dark psychology are traits within us all. We all contain the capacity for dark thoughts and actions and we all implement them to get what we want in a variety of ways and varying degrees. Have you never told a little lie to spare someone's feelings? Have you never omitted details to save yourself some skin? While these infractions seem usual and even banal in comparison to cyberstalking or child abduction, they all fall into that dark corner of psychology where the individual, from whatever stimuli or subjection, utilizes deception, illusions, fear, and manipulation to get what is wanted.

Narcissism, psychopathy, and Machiavellianism are the three classically studied personality types in dark psychology. These are frequently referred to as the dark triad.

Professor Del Paulhus coined this phrase in 2002 to refer to the three dark personalities we observe in the study of dark psychology. More recently, Paulhus has added a fourth to this list—the everyday sadist. Paulhus stresses the importance of professionals distinguishing these personalities where they very often get confused. Dr. Paulhus indicates the importance of proper categorization and labeling of these four personality types because each is unique and offers different insights that clumping will not suffice. This is particularly important in law enforcement, for example, to track down a criminal psychopath, like the Zodiac Killer, as opposed to a narcissist like Kanye West. Adler shines a light on the need for superiority and

Paulhus builds upon this key psychological theory.

The Four Dark Horses

It's true we all possess the capacity for these personality traits in ourselves to varying degrees but it can be tricky to see these qualities in ourselves. Surely someone comes to mind, whether from real everyday life or media, who is in love with themselves, appearances, and material wealth. Kim Kardashian? Your colleague? Your crush? Your parent? Batman? It's much easier to picture someone else you've been exposed to when considering these personality types.

When considering the following personality types, it should be noted that in many cases, all of these personality types can project themselves as very sociable and caring. These personality types are generally very good at making friends and making a good first impression. People even admire these individuals.

These types of people may be quiet, sly, and will already have you in a web of deceit before you recognize what's going on unless you know how to identify it first.

Narcissism

The individual with narcissistic tendencies is obsessed with the ego. Their favorite topic is themselves. This individual possesses an excessive and exaggerated interest and admiration for oneself and their physical appearance, and in general, how they appear to others. This is, as Adler would say, derived from a clear and powerful need for superiority over all others in their subjective experience. The narcissist doesn't enjoy getting to know the thoughts and emotions of others. It is unimportant to them why others feel the way they do. But if the narcissist is offered the platform to talk about why they feel the way they do, it will be at length. In fact, the narcissist will hijack a conversation when possible to speak about their own experiences in place of the experiences of other individuals. There is no use going to the root of something unless it is about them. The narcissist is impressed with material wealth, appearances, signs of success, and powerful people. Being average is the worst label to be assigned.

Several additional traits or behaviors may indicate you are dealing with a narcissist:

Manipulative - the individual manipulates information or scenarios in an attempt to ensure a path to the outcome they desire

Exploitive - the individual is quick to take advantage of or make use of others in order to gain the desired outcome

Critical of others - the individual commonly complains about the behaviors or accomplishments of others, especially those who disagree or are in opposition to themselves

Blame others - the individual never sees themselves at fault. If an undesirable outcome or mistake occurs, it is the effect of someone or something else. Narcissists are rarely accountable for their own mistakes.

The individual has high or unachievable expectations of others and often uses demanding language such as "you must", "have to", or "the only way". The individual does not manage conflict in a productive or healthy way. The conflict is seen as a contest and there can only be one superior winner. The outcome is almost inconsequential so long as the narcissist is perceived as the winner of the contest.

The individual exaggerates the qualities and accomplishments that they perceive as valuable in the eyes of others and tends to downplay or ignore the qualities or mistakes that may be considered inferior or weak. Portraying oneself in the perfect light is most important. The individual treats people around them with praise, gifts, and care when they want something but treat these same people with calloused hands and cruelty when others do not comply.

Victims of narcissists tend to be people who cannot initially read the individual well enough to spot the narcissistic behavior. This can easily be people with low self-worth or self-esteem who have a great need to gain approval or love from others.

Narcissists do not necessarily target a certain demographic. Age, sex, ethnicity, or religion matters not to the narcissist so long as the person is easily controlled without much emotional investment.

People who are easily isolated make good victims because they rarely have others around to question or challenge them and they typically do not have much going on in the outside world so they can give most of their attention to the narcissist. Those who quickly back down when confronted or criticized and those who are afraid to stand up for themselves make excellent targets.

Similarly, individuals who identify as empathetic, forgiving, emotional, and caring are often great targets to the narcissist. However, the narcissist also sees these traits as a sign of weakness and if the relationship becomes too complicated with these emotions, the narcissist will distance from that immediately in order not invest time and effort into the relationship for what they see as little to no return on the investment.

In short, the best target for a narcissist, as is the case with all of these dark personalities, is the person in need of something who is willing to give attention to them. If the person is easily controlled and does not require the narcissist to invest a deep amount of emotional effort, this abusive relationship can continue indeterminately until the narcissist feels as much has been taken as can be from the target.

Machiavellianism

The individual who exhibits Machiavellianism is so dedicated to the idea of superiority that they are willing to follow any means to the end they desire. This is most typically referenced in a political arena to mean someone willing to use any means necessary to gain or maintain political power.

So who is Machiavelli and what's the origin?

The early 1500s, Italy—Machiavelli is an accomplished politician from Florence. Machiavelli is thrust into a jarring and discordant time politically. Early in life, he represented and served political alignments faithfully but after years of exposure to the underhandedness and corruption of politics, he began to speak against it. Eventually, Machiavelli was removed from power and shunned. In his isolation, Machiavelli wrote what is now his best known political work, a collection of political writings called *The Prince*.

Like many of its time, *The Prince* is said to be a "mirror for the princes". Essentially, it is a prince's guide to politics—how to conduct oneself into a position of power, to be feared, not loved. *The Prince* calls for its readers to consider the use of all of the worst imaginable atrocities in order to gain and maintain power over others. Further, the reader is advised to combine all atrocities in one swift blow for maximum damage and control that will not be soon challenged. The point of *The Prince* is that political power is worth any and all means necessary to gain and keep power over all others.

The Prince was a bit of a different mirror, however. Though *The Prince* is remembered and even recited as a text in support of power by all means necessary, it is suggested that Machiavelli wrote this not in support of but in condemnation of the operations of politics as he had come to know it personally.

So while we have come to know the Machiavellian personality as the unscrupulous opportunist and schemer, the ironic reality is that Machiavelli himself tried desperately to expose the lack of morality and dignity rife within the system.

Those clever enough will understand Machiavelli's *The Prince* and are cautious as a result of taking the texts for their true meaning: a warning to others about their exploitation.

Psychopathy

The individual with psychopathic tendencies, unfortunately, combats a range of dangerous preconceived notions. Contrary to what Hollywood would have you believe, not all psychopathic personalities are chainsaw murderers and stalkers. Some of them are delivering your packages, cutting your deli meat, selling garden supplies, or taking your ticket stubs. On average, 1 in every 100 people has a psychopathic personality disorder, whether diagnosed or not.

A psychopathic personality is typically one that exhibits regular signs of antisocial thought or behavior. This is commonly accompanied by a deformed sense of empathy, remorse, and love. The individual who exhibits psychopathic behaviors is likely bold and uninhibited, proud of what they can get away with, and unmoved by consequences even if those consequences include pain or death. As you might surmise, these individuals are often (but not always) individuals who have long since experienced violent and sexual abuse and even long term mental and emotional abuse at the hands of others. This is often a subjective experience in childhood which afflicts the victim well into adulthood, often compounding and intensifying as time goes by.

Psychopaths are often (but again, not always) highly

intellectual and thus often board with others around them with whom they interact. Therefore, a sense of playing a game with others, and objectifying others rather than considering them as people, begins to take hold on the psychopathic personality. They take pleasure in thinking they've got the attention of someone with whom they can play mind games and control. A great example of this is Hannibal Lecter to Clarice Starling in the popular thriller *Silence of the Lambs.*

This reminds us that thanks to Hollywood and sensationalism, the word "psychopath" has taken on a skewed version of itself, in comparison to its less sensational and actual diagnosis.

We typically know psychopaths as killers, rapists, or pedophiles. While these (and other) traits are frequently present in the personalities of killers and rapists, the likelihood of psychopathy being nearer to you than the next pedophile is alarming but true. Psychopathic tendencies are marked by the individual's lack of feelings or remorse. Those studied are often reported to have "dead eyes" or "empty eyes", in many cases after having just committed gross atrocity but also just sitting across from in conversation. The closest psychopathic personality may make your coffee just the way you like it each morning. Or, it may be the next Timothy McVeigh.

Today, the debate remains strong as to whether the clinical psychopath actually receives benefit from counsel and therapy. Therapists often agree that therapy only gives a boost to the psychotic ego, allowing the psychopathic patient a platform to speak about themselves where the listener is ever present and focused on them.

Psychopaths see those who identify with empathy and forgiveness as below them—weak. Psychopaths are articulate and intellectual but not emotional. Emotional people who are openly caring and trusting are prime targets to the psychopathic personality. The psychopath sees these people as easily manipulated and exploitable.

Studies have shown that brain development of the psychopathic personality is different from that of the typical individual in that the psychopath often exhibits signs of a deformed amygdala, the part of the brain responsible for generating feelings like empathy and remorse. This deformed brain structure is also associated with the personality's tendency to exhibit no signs of revulsion to the violence or torture of others.

Psychopaths tend to show contempt and flippant regard in their body language more than the actual language. This is because psychopaths often believe they are clever enough to manipulate their language to persuade and convince others of a fact or reality. And to their credit, they are very often correct. They can manipulate and control others with language. But body language doesn't lie and though the words may be false, the body can be read for truth. This is even the case with those who think themselves cleverly above the rest.

Individuals looking to establish a representation of reality or a story to a target may blink an unusually high amount of times in telling the story. Similarly, they may keep their eyes closed for a prolonged time or blink very slowly during the parts of the story they know are not true. This is a basic tactic used by investigators to identify lies or omissions of truth.

The psychopathic personality often speaks in low and monotonic sounds that lack emphasis or emotion in parts of speech where this expression would be expected.

Look into the eyes of the person speaking to you. Are these the eyes of someone authentically expressing concern or are these eyes empty and dead? The psychopath's eyes are expressionless when the rest of the rehearsed face performs. A truthful person's eyes will align with their true intentions and passions.

Contempt collects at the corner of the mouth and when an individual corners their mouth, it is often a sign of contempt for the subject of conversation—exposed—though the speaker thinks it is hidden or means to expose it with a flare of sarcasm.

A dark personality will show blatant disregard for consequence, sure that they are clever enough to elude consequence or too superior to befall it. A person speaking with the face and nose tilted at an utmost angle are revealing their belief that they are better than who or what is being discussed.

Everyday Sadism

While sadists do share some traits and behaviors with the first three dark personality types, such as a grandiose perception of themselves or a lack of empathy for others, they differ in one major way. Their thoughts and behaviors are not always a way to manipulate others for a certain outcome. Instead, the sadist takes action against another simply for the pleasure of inflicting pain or cruelty.

As such, sadists can be easily drawn to jobs and careers that will allow them to practice this enjoyment freely or in a justified manner. Acting as a police officer or as a member of the military would be enticing for these individuals for the violence that could easily be served unto others. This is not to say that all who seek these jobs live with dark personality disorders. Of course, other personality traits like courage and selflessness are also attracted to jobs that allow them to help and protect those around them.

The Dark Singularity

Within the realm of dark psychology lurks an anomaly we thankfully do not meet with except under extremely rare circumstances. This is a dark personality whose cruel and deceptive behaviors have no real motivation or goal. The Dark Singularity represents this .01% of the population that, at least in theory, grows more and more heinous in behavior with no end in sight. The atrocities continue to escalate while any semblance of a motive drastically decreases.

Dark Communication

Now that we've taken a look at the classic personality types that exhibit distinct and significant levels of dark psychological tactics such as egomania, deception, and manipulation, we can more easily identify when less drastic versions of these behaviors drive us or those around us.

You may be able to detect this in yourself in the ways you interact with your colleagues or your neighbors. Though you may not take the dramatic steps a Machiavellian may take, you may detect a hint of deception or persuasion in trying to bring about a certain goal you have in mind.

Detecting these thought patterns and behaviors in yourself and others will benefit you in a number of ways, least of all to protect you and give you an edge over others, but it's not just about being able to detect these tactics. The real psychology begins when you communicate with others around you.

Verbal communication, language, voice—these are part of the powerful repertoire of instruments we use for communication but body language is in many cases a more revealing form of communication. There are many examples of words being deceptive and untrue, but the subconscious communication of the human body is rarely a liar.

As you have come to know the study of personalities on the dark side of psychology so, too, will you come to know the practice of deliberate and dark communication.

Broadcasting information to others and receiving the information others broadcast is where the magic lies.

Magic is really the right word for it, too. As Dr. Chris Cummings points out in a 2016 TedTalk in Singapore, communication is a lot like a magic spell. And as some of the greatest stories tell us, magic can be used for good or evil.

Communication is our magic power and with it, we can choose to communicate for the betterment of someone or something or for a greater benefit of social change. Or, we can use communication to fuel fear, hate, intolerance, and destruction.

As one of the most significant communicators of our time has on occasion said, it is *with great power [that] comes great responsibility.* It is our responsibility to understand better how to receive and broadcast information from one another. It is our duty to learn to use the instruments we are given to communicate deliberately. For our own protection, for the benefit of the ones we love, for the betterment of our societies, yes. But also, simply to get what we want. We can do this by using deliberate and subtle techniques of communication (both verbal and non-verbal) to help others see they really wanted what you wanted all along.

Dr. Cummings is currently the Assistant Professor of Strategic Communications at the Wee Kim Wee School of Communication and Information in Singapore. Dr. Cummings investigates and makes sense of communication, particularly "risk communication" and the impacts of deliberate and manipulative communication when it comes to critical decisions, personally, socially, or globally. He also talks about how to use communication as magic to get what you want.

For effective communication, we begin this process by putting an idea from one mind to another mind. If we oversimplify the process of communicating, we could say that communication is a translation of vibrations. Electrical impulses move from the brain to over 100 parts of the body to form speech. This speech comes out as sound waves. These sound waves are received and then are translated into specific sounds that represent words and ideas that hit inside another brain. Learning and implementing deliberate language and communication, then, is a responsibility to become proficient with our instruments. And you already know this: practice makes perfect.

To practice effective communication, the first key, again, is to move an idea from one mind to another. The very best way to move an idea into another mind quickly is by way of synesthetic ideation. This is just a fancy way to say we understand with our senses and our senses are connected in our minds. Our senses work together to form a representation of the world in our minds.

There is a simple but effective classic test Dr. Cummings references to illustrate this idea. In the 1920s, psychologists asked test takers to listen to the sound of two words. The test takers were then shown two shapes and asked to match each word with its shape. The two words were "kiki" and "boba". One shape was a star-like shape made of sharp edges and points. The other shape was an amoeba-like shape with soft and rounded sides. Can you guess which shape was called kiki and which was called boba?

Overwhelmingly, test takers did the obvious and assigned the word with rounded sound and letters and matched it to the rounded shape. Likewise, the sharper sounding word with pointed characters was assigned to the sharp and pointed shape.

Though a simple test, this helps to show that we use

several senses together to understand and draw inference from the world around us. Indeed, we gather information through sight, sound, smell, taste, and touch and if effective communication of an idea between two minds is to occur, the place to start is with as much sensory information as you can call upon to transmit the idea clearly.

When confronted with a stimulus, every organism exhibits affect. This can range from extremely basic such as we see in single-celled organisms, to extremely dynamic such as we see in the interactions of human beings. Whichever is the case, there is always an operation by which the organism processes the primal emotions and physiology of their stimulated state. Those who would seek to communicate with deliberate motivation are aware of the human effects and among the most powerful is fear.

Fear is a powerful emotion that links deeply to our instinct for survival. Fear helps to keep us and our offspring safe and alive. Fearful experiences great and small are also very visceral experiences from which we tend to draw and retain powerful sensory information. We recall these details as we move through life in hopes that they will help to protect us or mitigate our damages.

Imagine you are watching a video on YouTube. The video promises you'll see scary footage never seen before. But halfway through the video, a scary ghost face pops up with a screech and startles you. We all fall for it at least once and thinking of it now, the ghost face seems almost more annoying than terrifying. Yet, there was a brief moment, albeit a fraction of a second, in which the video did scare you enough to jump, to exclaim, and enough to cause a physical reaction in your body and send a rush of adrenaline through you or cause you to flinch. Your brain assessed the scenario in a split second, considering the surroundings and circumstances, and decided danger from the ghost face was not real. So you moan mildly annoyed or laugh as a way to process that emotion—that fear effect. But consider later tonight you are comfortable in your bed about to drift to sleep. You open your eyes ever so slightly as you turn over and you suddenly see the ghost face pop up in front of you. That's not so funny anymore.

The emotion of fear can be especially powerful information, particularly when the environment and circumstance are set deliberately with it in the communication. Perhaps nowhere is this more exploited than in news media.

Social Manipulation

It is in the UK news media of the 1980s that we find one famous example of utilizing fear and dark communication to create large scale widespread social manipulation all for the benefit of profit. Throughout the United Kingdom, an outbreak of infectious disease is discovered to be affecting cattle. Bovine spongiform encephalopathy is the name of the disease. BSE for short. But the problem is no one really cares. No one is interested in a mouthful of words that doesn't impact them in any felt way.

So a clever reporter with an innate sense of deliberate and persuasive language realized that instead of reporting on what the disease is, he should report on what it does. Thus, the disease came to be called mad cow disease.

The reporter took one, scary, highly unlikely scenario and linked it to our instinctual fear. Mad Cow Disease could, in rare cases, be transmitted to humans through the consumption of infected beef. Though the magnitude of this was quite high, the probability of this happening was extremely low. But this didn't matter because the high magnitude possibility was linked to our fears and we —globally—acted in accordance with those fears to such an extent that the entire global economy was impacted.

With a few deliberate changes to communications, the reporter was able to get people across the world to react in a very real and physical way that still lingers today. People paid attention en masse because of a well-planned fear response.

The trick is in getting people to be scared and then knowing when and how to calm them down again. We see this used in news tactics today with clickbait headlines like *5 Ways Your Daughter Will Die in Minutes if You Don't Do This*. It's any tactic that elicits fear as a means to get your mind and body to align perfectly with the goal they have in mind. This is the magic of deliberate communication.

Next, we take a look at a well known and widely used practice of using deliberate communication to bypass the logical mind and tantalize the imagination into complying with what you want.

If you find you've already learned new and valuable information that will help you, take a minute to return the favor and review this book online.

Design the Outcome You Want with NLP

Now we understand the inner workings of dark psychology and how it relates to the world that surrounds us. These darker psychological traits are used on us and by us in everyday life. These manipulative tactics vary from the mundane to the extreme and we find them in the small morning routine at the cafe as well as the televised and internationally significant meeting between one world leader and another.

Whether the objective is small or grand, we know that it's effective communication that will get your coffee made just how you like it. It's effective communication that will help leaders see common ground and agree to a compromise that suits all parties. We know that communication is most effective when all the senses are evoked and when imagery is used to elicit emotional responses like fear. Now we unpack the study of using structured and deliberate imagery and language to bring an outcome or idea to fruition. To start, we consider the widely used and highly effective process known as NLP or neuro-linguistic programming.

Let's break down the phrase. *Neuro*, in this case, refers to our human nervous system. *Linguistic* refers to language; the use of language. *Programming* is usually the most familiar term and in this case, refers to information scheduled and trained in a particular way. With neuro-linguistic programming, we are looking at the use of language to trigger the nervous system to behave in a scheduled, methodical way. This is accomplished in the self as well as other individuals, or masses of people.

Neuro-Linguistic Programming is the study and practice of using the mind and the body to organize perceptions and behaviors in a way that produces a certain result. This result can be achieved through the control of another or through the control of oneself. In fact, a significant proportion of the NLP practiced is applied to oneself for the retraining and refining of one's own thoughts, actions, and reactions to the stimuli of the world. As we've already seen, we use our sensory perception to build an internal map of the world we move through, establishing what is possible and impossible. Our senses go about organizing information on the map. We use this map to run through scenarios and test information for decision making. At some point in the process, we actually stop responding to the actual stimuli of the world and we start reacting to the map of what we think the reality is. Our thoughts and behaviors become conditioned responses to events on the map. But if that map could be edited then the mind and body could be retrained to act differently for a benefit or purpose. Here's a secret: the map can be edited.

Before we delve deeper into our maps of reality, we should back up to a significant moment in historic psychology and social communication for a better understanding of how information is broadcasted and received.

Milton Erickson and His Map

Milton Erikson's contribution is important to note at this point because it strengthens our overall understanding of several suggestive ideas that play a major role in the application of neuro-linguistic programming.

First, Erickson understood the power of metaphor and storytelling. Invoking the power of images, and ultimately, the imagination is the most reliable and effective tool a therapist has to offer his patient. Second, Erickson supported the idea that by tapping into the unconscious mind, the patient could generate and access solutions to issues which could not be accessed by the conscious critical thinking mind. Third, Erickson taught several very powerful methods still used in psychotherapy (and NLP) today that take the patient from an analytical state of mind to a freer and more creative unconscious state. Arguably the most important aspect of these techniques in the use of "trance", which is the basis for all hypnotic therapies used today.

Milton Erickson was born at the end of 1901 in Aurum, a small mining community in eastern Nevada, which is now a deserted ghost town. Growing up in Wisconsin, Erickson had every intention of continuing the family farming business but a series of seemingly unfortunate events changed the course of his life. As a young child, Erickson developed and overcame color blindness and dyslexia, through what Erickson claims was his own mind's unconscious power. He later wrote about these experiences in his academic paper called Autohypnotic Experiences of Milton H. Erickson. As a young man, Erickson again encountered physical ailments that would keep him from the fields and farm work. Such a severe case of polio set into Erickson that doctors were sure he would die.

Instead of dying, Erickson, who suffered so much he could not even speak, was inspired to program his mind to recall memories, images, and sensations of when his muscles had been working. With literally nothing else he could do, Erickson took control of the one function he could reach—thought. After a slow and dedicated practice, Erickson moved from sure death to regaining speech and even the use of his arms. Still facing the paralysis of his legs, Erickson took drastic action to shock his body back into action. Without the use of his legs, Erickson set out on a canoe adventure over a thousand miles long. Alone. By the completion of his journey, he could walk again, though he used the assistance of a cane.

Not surprisingly, the experiences of Erickson's traumas from younger life directed him to an intense curiosity of medicine and psychology. Erickson was a successful medical student but could not stay away from the magic of the mind and he spent more and more time in the study of psychology and psychiatry. It's his work in these initiatives that he is so well known for and frequently referenced.

Erickson swings back toward the psychoanalytic work of Freud, from Adler. Erickson recognized the sum parts of the individual, but he, like Freud, believed in the ability and benefit of separation of personality components. While Freud coined these aspects of separation the id, the ego, and the superego, Erickson took a different approach and separated not the personality components but the state of the brain: conscious, subconscious, and unconscious. He maintained that by confusing the conscious mind, he could access the solution-generating imagination of his patients. In a trancelike state, Erickson's patients would become highly creative, imaginative, and highly suggestible in a way that would override the information stored in the mind's conscious map of reality. These seeds planted by Erickson in the earlier part of the 20th century have grown into the garden of neuro-linguistic programming. We fast forward to the 1970s where we find the gardeners of NLP, Richard Bandler and John Grinder.

Richard Bandler and John Grinder

Both Bandler and Grinder studied and majored in psychology in California in the 1960s. Grinder, in fact, earned his doctorate in linguistics in New York City and soon after took a position as the assistant professor of linguistics at the University of California, Santa Cruz. It was at this same university that Bandler was completing his BA in philosophy when their paths crossed and changed the face of communication again.

Bandler and Grinder had both spent much of their time dissecting the operations and patterns of linguistics and both we heavily influenced by similar schools of thought in psychology. Both too were influenced by similar philosophical (and even spiritual) ideas. The two men were subsequently introduced to Milton Erickson himself while he was still practicing and teaching the therapeutic techniques and theories to younger generations of psychologists and counselors.

Together, the three professionals embarked on a study of language that produced a set of words and techniques that when used systematically were an extremely effective communication to persuade others rapidly. These techniques, now referred to as NLP, are used across many industries in addition to psychology because they are so exceptionally effective. Sales forces, politicians, police officers, lawyers, and entertainers, just to name a few, are all industrious professionals who come into regular contact with the operations of neuro-linguistic programming. Whether this application is intentional or indirect, there is no denying that effective and persuasive communication is a major part of the role.

Based in the earlier works of Erickson, Bandler and Grinder suggest there is an undeniable network between the language we broadcast, the translations made in the mind, and the behavior patterns we've adopted because of this. Further, Bandler and Grinder suggest that by controlling the language and the translation that occurs, we can alter the behaviors. Let's see how it works.

Key Ideas to Master NLP

3 Central Concepts

The works of Bandler and Grinder revolve around three major concepts. The first major concept we must accept is that the individual experiences the world subjectively. Though we both may see the same car accident occur, my experience of the event will undoubtedly be different from yours. We have each share similar points of reference but each individual's experience is registered uniquely in the brain. What registers can depend on any and all factors of subjective experience up until this point for the individual. We each have our own unique perception of the world, whether factually accurate or not.

The second major concept is that the mind is actually the sum of a conscious and unconscious mind, each serving the individual in distinct ways. It is possible to suspend or bypass the conscious critical thinking mind in order to access the subconscious (or unconscious) mind. When the unconscious mind is accessed, and a highly suggestible state is induced, the mind can be programmed to achieve the desired outcome. This is used in the training of sales teams and community leaders, as well as therapeutically with a patient to overcome some issue, like a phobia, for example.

The third major concept is called modeling. Modeling is what Bandler and Grinder call the practice of recreating the excellence of one individual within another individual, regardless of expertise or activity. A sales professional who experiences trouble closing the deal can learn to be an excellent closer by modeling the thought and behavior patterns of an already excellent closer.

With these three concepts under our hat, we can move onto what is commonly referred to as "the four pillars of wisdom" within the study of NLP.

4 Pillars of Wisdom

The four pillars of NLP are meant to point out that though some of us are moving along and achieving success and happiness, we are using but a smidge of the power we truly have to surpass our goals and exceed our expectations. We may think we have a good idea of what we want but is that accurate? Many times we think we set a terrific positive goal for ourselves. We feel enthusiastic about doing the work it takes to get there.

We are filled with anticipation for what it will feel like to complete the goal. We are ecstatic about soon reaping the benefits and having the change we so badly want.

Too often, our goals are too loosely set. We forget to specify when the goal should be met. Putting a deadline on a goal increases your odds of holding yourself accountable and working away at it a little at a time. It's often said that a goal without a deadline is just a dream. We also forget to define some way of knowing when the goal is met. The goal can be to build a home but how are you to know when to call the goal complete? When the last wall is up? When all the paint is dry? When the furniture is just right, or maybe the garden, the yard? A similar problem occurs in online marketing frequently. The online business wants to put up a new lead to funnel sales and prospects. "I want more leads" is the goal. This is not good enough; it's too loose. Do you really want more leads or more valuable customers from the leads? This might mean implementing a different approach that will ultimately attract fewer leads but a higher quality return customer. The point is that the goal is too vague. Define when the house is considered done. Define what "more leads" really means. There should be a measurement which can be held against the goal to say when it is successfully complete. That's not to say you can never add another window or wall to the house. It's not to say this will be your last lead funnel ever. More than likely, if your first goal is managed well and accomplished you will have more goals in mind you wish to set.

Another area of goal-setting challenge that slows us down is the actual, physical, action. Doing the little work to achieve a big goal. Think of the fate of just about any New Year's resolution. And why? We set the goal. We write it down. We put it in the calendar. Maybe we even invite others to join because we need the accountability buddy. But the calendar reminder pops and we just didn't get enough sleep. The accountability buddy texts you but you have to bail for today. Life happens and gets in the way. Sometimes we can't control the circumstance but sometimes we can and we just let other things take priority as an excuse. One thing is certain, whichever action you take most leads you to the outcome you will have most. So if you set a goal to run a marathon but you spend most of your training time binge-watching Netflix shows, you will be a super-knowledgeable master of the new sessions of shows, with no marathon finish time. Don't set the goal and walk away. Define the goal. Set time in your day for the goal. Keep the appointment.

When we have a goal in mind, it can be common to go tunnel-vision on the goal and put up blinders for everything else going on around us. This is not the behavior of a master of his program. A master knows that when a goal is set and the train is in motion, now is one of the most highly opportune times to keep peripheral vision sharp. Every second the goal is moving along is another opportunity for greatness or challenge to interfere. If your blinders are up, you will miss signs for shortcuts and warnings about falling rocks. This means as a goal-setter, you need to be aware of and receptive to the information and resources coming at you in every direction. This doesn't mean you should be deterred and always be changing directions. The stimuli are there to help you along, not to distract you. Don't go in every direction but do be aware of what is in your path, and what moves in your vicinity that has the potential to cross your tracks, for better or worse. Practice engaging all of your senses it relates to the goal so that you can gain an adept reading of everything in your surroundings; your resources. But maintain your control. The stimuli should not shock you. Instead, use them each as a method of practice for maintaining your calm in the face of whatever weather. Be aware of your circumstances but do not let them control the roll of your train.

Adaptation is a vital skill for survival in many of life's situations and the same is true here. A goal needs to be clear, yes, but not unmovable. Exercising your ability to adapt and bend is going to serve you well in goal-setting, too. While you should have clear and measurable outcomes and records for your goals as you move along, you must be able to adapt to the changing terrain. Our moving train must be able to wind around the corners, cross the bridges, climb the mountains and switch tracks. If our train is not flexible enough to adapt to these changes in the environment, it plunges off the tracks. You have to be willing to accept that sometimes the due date will change. That's okay; just set a new one. Sometimes, the resources change. That's okay; your eyes are open wide enough to see the new potentials. Sometimes the tracks are out up ahead. That's okay; you have the tools to fix the tracks yourself, even if that means persuading someone else to fix them. There is always a way for the path to keep flowing but it is when you block yourself off and box yourself in that you stop the flow. The river knows the way to the ocean; you don't need to steer it or guide it. You just need to ride it.

Understanding and implementing these four principles helps the individual to maximize the outcome and benefits of a goal, and thus, to maximize one's quality of life. For each goal you set, practice these four pillars of wisdom:

- Every goal, regardless of how large or small, must have specifically designed parameters; a defined measurement for success, a deadline, there should be little or no ambiguity

- Every goal needs effort; action, and specifically a strategy that aligns with the goal

- Every goal will be affected by the individual's level of sensitivity to the world and its stimuli

- Every goal will be affected by the individual's capacity to adapt to changes in the plan

Gather Abundant Resources

As a practitioner of neuro-linguistic programming and persuasive conversation, it is important to gain as much insight and as many resources about the situation as you reasonably can. Sometimes you will have time to do your homework and dive into an investigation beforehand. Other times you will have to operate on the fly. Practice both. There is ample opportunity. Gather one or two key pieces of information the next time you're at a business meeting. Do this covertly, of course, by registering the body language around you or by looking what's missing; what's not being said at this meeting and why. How then can you use that information to persuade others to see your side at this meeting? This is a practical exercise to test your resourcefulness on the fly. In keeping with the same general arena, surely you know of some bigger meeting or event that's on the horizon. It needs your attention and discipline. So starting now, practice your long-term resourcefulness and see what you can gather over the lifespan of the preparation or project. There may be patterns of behavior you are able to see that you were blind to before. For example, over the course of a project, you may find that a colleague has a habit of being very disagreeable and short-tempered by the end of the week. For whatever reason, this habit unintentionally spills over into your project progress and it's slower going when working with this person at the end of the week. At the start of every week, this person exhibits stellar performance. If you weren't paying better attention you might not notice the pattern and only come to think of the person as disagreeable. But since you've noticed the pattern of information (a resource!) you are able to use that information to pivot and plan your project better. Maybe you can help the person, maybe you work around them, maybe you have to let them go from the project but whatever you do, you now have a piece of information on which to base your next move. If you can do this with one small piece of information, imagine what you can do with the resources you pick up when you really start to pay attention.

Paying attention in order to gain resources is vital if you are trying to change or program something about yourself. If you want to program yourself to wake up earlier so you can study for an important upcoming exam, you may want to observe and take note of details like: what do I feel like upon just waking up? Do I wake peacefully or am I scared awake by my alarm clock? Do

I get out of bed right away or do I tend to lay awake for a few minutes, thinking about the day to come? Take note of whether you have a morning bathroom and preparation routine; if you like to eat by a certain time. Take note of how you feel when you're studying for the exam. Do you have a conducive study zone? Is your heart rate fast or slow? Do you feel a particular emotion or does your body react physiologically in some way? Take note of when and how you start to lose focus in your studies and whether it might help to have someone study with you. Paying attention to all these smaller pieces of information about yourself and your habits pay off when you put together the bigger picture and plan your goal. With all this extra insight, you can now do your very best to plan the most effective path to your goal. You know you will need to combat that 10 minutes of laying in bed with a jumpstart of incentive. You know you'll need to drive to the library because your house is too distracting a place to concentrate in the morning. You know you'll need to plan to stand and stretch every 30 minutes so you don't lose focus. Or whatever the case may be. The point is that by paying attention to these details and by gathering these resources, you are able to set your goal and accomplish it faster and easier, and you start to develop excellent goal-setting (and goal accomplishing) skills that will continue to serve you better for the rest of your life.

Paying attention to the benefit of others works in much the same way. It takes your focus on the circumstances as they relate to the other person and the other person's goal. Because you know your own inner workings better than you can know another's it takes quieting your own self and listening to the other. Where you would normally watch for an emotion or a physiological reaction from yourself, you must now be aware of that in the other person. You must be able to discern well enough if a piece of information is coming from them or if you have filtered it with bias. A personal coach might ask his client about topics that do not directly relate to the client's goals or goal-setting behaviors. Instead, the coach is catching clues from the client candidly. The client perceives the small-talk questions about the weekend's shenanigans is just that - small talk. The client doesn't realize the coach is gathering resources covertly. The coach pays attention to the clients' expressions and body language. The coach watches when the clients look down and to the side to remember what someone said or did. The coach notes when the clients speak with fervor and enthusiasm and when the clients cross their legs and speak with more hesitation and caution. Gathering this information is going to make it so much easier to help the client set goals and coach them to the finish line.

Resourceful information is not gathered once. A smart gatherer knows that an initial count of stock must be taken and then regularly monitored for changes. Factors are always changing and recalibrations are routinely necessary. Take an assessment of the situation at a given set of marks that are appropriate for your project. Review all of your resources, both literally and figuratively, each every given period; every season, every quarter, every week, every meal. Some resources will stay beside you the entire journey. Others will drop away. Still, others will bloom.

Whether the goal is long-term or short, whether the goal is yours or someone else's, the practitioner is ever-cognizant of the bigger picture and continually digging for resources to utilize. The words that are used, the tone and the breath, the heart rate, the posture, the smile. All of these details are being taken in with the deliberate intent of sculpting the desired outcome. Each bit of information is a lever, a screwdriver, a hammer, and a nail in the toolbox of practical persuasive linguistics.

A Confusion State

For an effective suggestion to be planted in the mind of the patient, it is imperative that the practitioner bypass the conscious critical mind and access the unconscious mind. For this bypass to take place and last long enough, an induction from beta brainwave to alpha (or theta) brainwave must occur and then deepen in trance. The quickest and most effective method for this induction is to introduce a confusion tactic that will interrupt the patient's usual pattern of behavior and register as a change on their internal map of reality. A simple but clear example of this is one very commonly used in NLP and stems from a method Erickson himself used—the Handshake Method.

Imagine you are introduced to Erickson. You both begin to extend your hands in what would be the usual social behavior in this or any similar "meet and greet" circumstance. But at the last second, instead of gripping your hand for a shake, Erickson gently grabs and holds your wrist for a brief moment. This subconsciously catches you off guard. In this instance, your internal map of reality is adjusted to fit for all the times a handshake occurred except that one time a wristshake occurred instead. A new mark on the map. The next time Erickson really wants the attention of your subconscious mind, he need only gently grab and hold your wrist for a moment to gain it. This is crossing the threshold from the attention of the conscious mind to the unconscious mind.

A Trance State

With the threshold crossed, now the practitioner must, to some degree, remain there. The quickest and most effective method for this is to maintain a trancelike state for the patient. While Hollywood may have you cautious of the word trance, it's not as scary as its made to sound. Inducing a trance state, in the case of NLP and hypnosis, is to assist the patient with the natural transition from beta brainwaves to alpha (and eventually theta) brainwaves. This is a process that every human naturally cycles through every day. Beta brain waves are what we operate on most of the time; when we are driving, cooking, watching Netflix. These are the thoughts and behaviors of someone operating on their internal map of reality and not necessarily on the actual stimuli or circumstance of the immediate environment.

Alpha brain waves occur when you snap out of that beta state and into an immediately engaged state of mind. For example, you are driving and thinking about something else entirely, rolling along, thinking in beta, and suddenly, a deer runs in front of your vehicle! Your brain waves move immediately from beta to alpha in order to best deal with the sudden scenario. Later that night, at home in your bed, you are drifting to sleep, eyes closed and breathing slow relaxed breaths. Just before you slip into your sleeping and dreaming state, your brainwaves shift to theta. It is actually in this theta state, which occurs just before and just after sleep, where suggestions are the most powerful.

The Power of Metaphor

There are many ways to communicate ideas effectively from one mind to another and we do this all the time. Most of this information, however, is temporary information that is held in the mind for as long as it is useful and then let go. The clerk at the convenience store might remember which packs of cigarettes her regulars ask for and maybe she has it ready before they even ask. The clerk doesn't typically hold onto this information for the one person passing through the state, whom she will never see again, which happened into the store. In and out the conscious mind. Then there is the subconscious mind. This is the fertile valley of limitless possibility. If you can get past the conscious mind and plant seeds in the subconscious mind, they will grow without resistance or restriction.

The best way to penetrate the rich soil of the subconscious mind is with a little story. Metaphor, and especially stories, are probably our oldest and most effective means of transitioning information from one person to another, and from one generation to another. We still hold onto stories that are thousands of years old, with complete conviction, because stories are so effective. Our minds, for a very long time, has made good use of organizing information. The way we know best to do this is by organizing information into a story. We understand it best, we remember it most consistently when there is a story the information is built into. The story is a pattern we cannot help but organize. All the random information that occurs in your mind as you sleep and dream is organized into a story format when you wake. Because the story is so strong within our species and our consciousness, we can utilize this information. Rather than struggle against human nature, use it. It works and you know what they say to leave it alone if it ain't broke. Use the power of metaphor and the power of story to support the goal you're serving.

It's said that there are really only three or fours kinds of stories that truly exist. Arguably, the great comedy, the great tragedy, the great adventure, and the great metamorphosis. Every other story is just a copy in a different cloak. So we can use these basic story forms to take the subconscious mind on an imagination ride. In whichever form suits best, take the hero on his journey. Devise a story to help the subconscious experience the desired outcome. If you're even just a little familiar with writing or storytelling, you've probably heard of Joseph Campbell and the Hero's Journey. If you're not familiar, it's worth taking a side path and getting to know this man and his ideas. Joseph Campbell offers a comprehensive and clear breakdown of metaphor and story and the agents of this communication. Familiarizing with the Hero's Journey will make your metaphor exceptionally sharp for all the places you intend to use them.

With subtle access to the subconscious mind through the use of metaphor, the mind will accept ideas and suggestions without resistance as an imagination. Because the suggestions were made at a highly susceptible time, the individual will be profoundly affected by the words and can more easily move to the desired outcome without restriction, too.

With these keys truths about metaphor in mind, neuro-linguistic programming says, "Let's use that". If stories are so relatable and potent, let's use them to establish deliberate marks on the internal map of reality.

Customizing the Map

We know that our internal map of reality is being mapped by a symphony of our senses. This map tells us quickly, based on previous experience, what we can expect to happen if a certain action is taken (or avoided). With this internal map, we are able to judge situations more quickly and with a better guess at risk and reward. This helps keep us alive as we move through a three-dimensional world of ever-changing stimuli. Though we may be impressive at mapping trillions of bits of data, we aren't always so accurate. Our map is more "middle-of-the-road"; more of what is generally possible. People don't "generally" climb that high on the mountain. It doesn't mean you can't. It doesn't mean people don't because you know they do sometimes. So the good news is, the map is very flexible and built to scale. We can update the map whenever we want with just a little effort and care.

Let's take the example of our distant ancestors meeting one vicious lion at night falls. The moment is tense and dangerous but our ancestor survives and the map marks that lion as dangerous. The next time our ancestor sees a lion, it doesn't take as long to recognize the risk and get away from that situation fast thanks to the map. But as we know, we end up acting based upon the information on the map and not the real-world possibilities. So it takes our ancestor a while to override the map and become a lion tamer. The lion tamer is a map changer.

We change the map with deliberate and specific language that uses metaphor and the individual's own beliefs and senses to imagine the desired scenario through a story. With persuasive techniques and the systems and formulas of NLP, we set a stage for success that will face no resistance. We customize and expand the map. Now the mind has experienced a new scenario and we have programmed the desired outcome. The more this pattern is rehearsed, the more detailed the map becomes, and the more likely it is for the individual to find their way to the outcome in the real world. This is because the individual now holds the capacity to imagine an outcome where the desire is possible and because we have changed the map (with repetition). The subconscious mind, and therefore the individual's body, is now able to act in accordance with one possibility or the other (or a new possibility). The possibility which is rehearsed the most is likely to be the outcome in real life.

Whether it is yourself or someone else, get down to the subconscious mind and hypnotize it with a story about itself. Ensure this story gets repeated consciously and subconsciously for the individual. Every trip down this path helps to pave the way and make the path a stronger reality.

3 NLP Techniques to Learn and Practice

The following are some of the most popular techniques used in NLP. There are many techniques and more are being developed all the time by famous practitioners like Paul McKenna and Tony Robbins. The techniques shared here, however, are among those with the greatest results amongst professionals, the most attention to academic study, or the widest used in psychotherapy.

Remember that while these techniques can sometimes seem like magic, it's real life application and practice that makes them so effective. Don't expect to plant a suggestion once and walk away with a met goal. While this is technically possible in some cases of hypnotherapy, it's repetition and reinforcement that will serve the practitioner best.

Modeling

We've learned that modeling is one of the three central concepts to the neuro-linguistic programming that Bandler and Ginder teach. We understand modeling in the broad sense of modeling one's thought and behavior patterns to mimic those of another who holds the success and expertise desired. A common example of this might be that we want to become a successful entrepreneur so we study the ideas and behaviors of one of our favorite entrepreneurs to follow. We see that this individual wakes at 4:30am every day to attend and complete a CrossFit workout session. We begin to model this behavior in ourselves in expectation of achieving our own entrepreneurial successes.

Modeling is not only one of three central concepts to the whole of NLP but it is also probably the most used technique and perhaps the most important skill to develop as a practitioner. The idea of modeling is deceptively simple sounding: see positive and beneficial behavior, copy it. But just how do you organize that into a structure you can apply consistently, measure, test, and analyze? While it may take some extra time and effort to think about your goals and techniques ahead of time, we don't want to overthink it or overcomplicate it either. Simple is safe and the simplest may be to just ask and watch. If you want to be a better business owner, ask other business owners what they do, watch them do it, and take measures to repeat those tasks or behaviors yourself on a regular basis.

We can model a desired behavior in the imagination as well. This is a powerful technique and is used very often in hypnosis for weight loss or smoking cessation. In a highly suggestible state, the individual's imagination is stoked with the idea of the scenario and behavior they want to modify and the outcome they desire. For example, let's say this individual wants to stop smoking. Using as much sensory information and resource as possible to draw from, we guide the individual through this vicarious experience. The individual is asked to describe their experience leading up to the desire for a cigarette. They are guided through the process of taking out a cigarette from the box; taking note of the sound of the experience, the smell, the weight of the cigarette between the fingers. The individual is guided through all the sensory details of the experience. They recall the feeling of stress before lighting, and then the relief they feel on the first inhale. We might stop here and model the experience with a new replacement behavior. For example, the individual is looking for a sense of relief upon smoking so choosing a behavior which will also elicit feelings of relief will be an excellent replacement. Let's say this individual also feels a great sense of peace and relaxation each time they hold a particular yoga pose for a moment. The individual is asked to run through the scenario but when they get to the strong feelings of stress or frustration, they are asked to model the new behavior instead. This time, the individual imagines standing up to go outside but not to smoke— to stretch. The individual is guided through all the sensory perceptions of moving in the yoga pose, holding it, feeling it stretch and expand their spine and ribs, and feeling the electric calm wash over them. This should be repeated several times in the imagination of the individual and then applied in real life. The next time the individual feels that familiar stress and frustration, is it as easy and satisfying to go outside for a stretch rather than a smoke?

Modeling is very often used in conjunction with other techniques such as anchoring or aversion therapy to maximize benefits and results. Because modeling is a foundation piece of the overall study, it's easy to understand how so many adaptations and combinations of it exist in hypnosis and psychotherapy today.

Modeling is a great technique to use for just about any goal you can imagine. It's particularly effective for use on oneself or in therapeutic or counseling work but it's easy to see this applied to common everyday experiences like that of a salesperson trying to put you into a brand new vehicle to drive away in. A clever salesperson might reach for access to the buyer's imagination by walking the buyer through the sensory experience of getting into their old car that knocks and grinds. It doesn't smell new, not enough elbow room, and that annoying blind spot. Then that salesperson might walk the buyer through the vicarious experience of driving away in a clean new car that only makes a sexy revving sound. That buyer may be more inclined to buy than before.

Anchoring

The next most referenced and applied technique used in neuro-linguistic programming is a powerful favorite from Milton Erickson's works directly—anchoring. Anchoring, essentially, is conditioning an individual for a certain response based on a sensory trigger such a handshake, an eyebrow moment, or a sound. Remember Pavlov and his dogs? We call it conditioning but it is the bell which is the anchor, a sensory trigger that is used to elicit a particular response. This is an excellent technique for use with someone you've only just met, as well as someone you've known for a while. For example, it may be your first time meeting with the person doing your job interview but you definitely want to make sure this person knows you're the right one for the position. Or, perhaps you are the manager of a sales team you've been working with for a few years now and it's important for them to learn a new operation. In both cases, anchoring could be used to maximize the power of your persuasion.

Let's look at the latter example first. In this case, you want the team you manage to accept the new operational changes and adhere to them. Lucky for you, your team goes "hands all in" at the end of each meeting, chanting a hail to their team and comrades. Hands-all-in with a quick team chant is doubly as good because it includes a sense of touch and sound. There is already a positive emotion attached to it. It's the perfect anchor resource. When you call your meeting for this operational change, consider starting with a "hands all in" to immediately create that general feeling of teamwork and comradery and subtly install the idea that this task is going to take all of us adapting and working together.

Let's look at the first example where you are just sitting down to your job interview with the interviewer for the first time and first impressions are everything. You specifically want to make sure this person knows you are great in a leadership position. You know leadership is crucial to this role and the highest priority for the interviewer. Anchoring can work well for you here in a rapid and subtle way. In your conversation about job responsibilities, lead the interviewer to talk about the importance of leadership in this role or company. Guide them to expand on why they so badly need a strong leader, or what paint points have come from poor leadership, or no leader. Pay attention to the interviewer's pace, tone, breathing, and body language as you listen. Find the points in their explanations when they mention, for examples, the traits of a leader they are looking for. When these traits are mentioned or described, raise your eyebrows in a subtle way that still makes sense in the conversation but it is subconsciously seen by the interviewer. Each time these precious qualities are mentioned or described, you are subtly and subconsciously anchoring them with the movement of your eyebrows.

A master at the craft of reading others may go the extra mile. Upon meeting the interviewer for the first time, the master would notice through language and body language that the interviewer is not one to make much eye contact in which case an eyebrow anchor would be lost. On the other hand, the master can deduce that while the interviewer does not much care for eye contact, he is a very auditory person. The master adapts at the last minute, substituting the eyebrow anchor for the click of a pen at the mention of these desired leadership qualities. Later, when the interviewer asks you to expand on your leadership skills and experience, you can utilize that visual or auditory trigger to subconsciously link yourself to the desired traits in the mind of the interviewer.

The trick here is paying attention to which emotional state you're setting your trigger. You don't accidentally want to set up a trigger each time an undesirable experience or quality is mentioned so that the interviewer later links you to those undesirable traits. Pay attention to the interviewer's emotions shifts and guide them to talk about the ideas that make them excited, happy, and cause them to smile. Though you may be talking at the moment about the specific task of being a leader, if the interviewer is feeling and experiencing the doubt and frustration of finding the right leader, you do not want to use this moment for an anchor. It would better suit you to use the moment the interviewer is arbitrarily telling you about how good the free lunch perks are because this is what the interviewer is also excited about. The words don't have to be exactly when you anchor, it's the emotional experience and state that is most important.

If you ever watch Tony Robbins giving a motivational speech, you will notice one of the physical anchors he has given himself and continues to use. You will see Robbins bump his hands to his chest in an enthusiastic and competitive expression. This for

Robbins is a physical trigger which is attached to intense feelings and sensory memories of mastery, power, and ecstasy. Each time he does this to himself, it's like giving himself a boost of that all-powerful nothing-can-stop-me-now feeling.

Reframing

Another often used core aspect of neuro-linguistic programming is the reframing technique. As with the first two techniques, this is so versatile and effective it's great for use with programming oneself and in helping and persuading those around you. Reframing is another one of these techniques that we naturally just do. The problem is we usually do it exactly wrong and end up hurting ourselves instead of helping.

Think of an arbitrary occurrence. There is traffic ahead and you're all stuck in it. Your friend is driving but the movement is a crawl in both directions. People are hot, tired, and frustrated. Somewhere in the back of the line, a truck honks loud and long. Your friend suddenly reacts as if the horn was directed at her personally. After shooting off a mouthful of names and offenses at the honker in the truck, your friend sits and stews about the scenario. Maybe she plays it back and forth in her head thinking of what she should have said if it's too late to say it now. This is where we go wrong with reframing. We egocentrically settle into the idea that the environment revolves around us and everyone's watching and listening and every mishap is done to us. It's almost as if they are doing it to us on purpose. And yet that is ridiculous. In all probability, the honking had nothing at all to do with your friend and while she could have reframed it in a positive way that made her feel better, she, like most of us, reframed it negatively and dwelt in the bad feelings of that imagining.

Good news. You know NLP and you can help your friend reframe this positively instead of negatively in this critical psychological moment. When you sense the downward spiral, pull your friend back up and out. Help her reframe in a positive way. That means, in a way that makes her feel at least neutral toward the circumstance and at best, happy about the temporary condition.

Help to expand your friend's internal map of reality. Cut through the critical analytical thought and straight to her imagination. Help her to imagine another possibility. Help your friend to see that it is likely the honk is not directed at her. What if the honk was honked because the driver is not mad at anyone at all but simply has to go to the bathroom quite badly. Your friend, through your swift reframing of the situation, can lessen the stress and resistance she feels by imagining she is likely not the subject of the offense. She feels silly for being mad at the poor horn honker in the first place.

Reframing is an excellent practice for regaining feelings of control and power in a moment that may initially strum feelings of frustration or powerlessness for you or your friend. Remember to reframe a negative emotion with a neutral or humorous one. The replacement should feel good, not worse. If you don't feel perfect about your first attempts to reframe, don't give up. It takes some practice just as the rest of the techniques do. If there is resistance in a statement used for reframing, try augmenting the statement, or generalizing the statement more, to lessen the resistance.

Pick a technique and try it on yourself for about 30 days. Be clear about the goal you have it mind and how you will know it is a success when the deadline comes. Record your experiences and results and try this again for another 30 days, with the same goal, and adjustment of the goal, or a completely new goal (congratulations if you've achieved the first goal). Record your experiences and results again. When you are comfortable with the process, you can experiment with this technique on others in your everyday life. Which routine scenarios do you experience that would make an excellent testing ground? Play with a more deliberate and subtle language when speaking with others.

245

Now that you are aware of the methods and benefits of retraining the brain, let's look at how to make life easier by getting others to agree with you and do what you want.

Persuasion, Manipulation, and Coercion

Persuasion and manipulation are two very similar ideas. In fact, these two exclusive ideas are often mixed and the lines between them begin to blur. How do we tell the difference between persuasion and manipulation, and are these really dark qualities? If we consider the definition of the two words we begin to see a difference. The difference is in the motivation. While this can easily start to sound a bit unethical, consider this may be due to your exposure to the sensationalism of persuasion or manipulation.

When we talk about these two topics in movies, on talk shows, on Facebook, there is quite often a negative component. Someone has been taken advantage of by way of being persuaded or manipulated. But that might actually be a bit of a minor miscommunication with words. Instead of being persuaded or manipulated, the victim may have actually been coerced.

This can be thought of in a similar light of the expression, "I'm so jealous!" Media has warped the meaning of the word jealous just as the word persuasion has been warped. Jealousy denotes the specific quality of wanting what someone else has and wanting that they do not have it. Specifically, they do not have it. If you have an apple and I am jealous, I want to have that apple and I don't want you to have any apples. When someone says they're jealous, this is not usually what they mean. What is really meant is, "I'm so envious!"

I'm glad you have the apple but I want one, too.

The terms persuasion and manipulation have fallen to a similar, confused state when they are not necessarily used how they are intended. Persuasion, when you look at it alone and unfiltered, is not such a scary idea. In fact, it's downright natural. Persuasion is the act of leading another to believe something and/or to act upon this belief.

Leading others to believe something does not inherently mean the persuasion is negative. We use persuasion in myriad ways every day to navigate the world and cope with ever-changing circumstances. A wife may persuade her husband that the vacation they really want this year is Bali, not another trip to Miami. A child on the playground may persuade a friend to trade one Pokemon card for another. The teacher persuades the class to sit down. The veterinarian persuades the puppy to sit still. The store clerk persuades you to get one more; it's cheaper in bulk. The CDC persuades everyone to stay inside and seal the windows.

These persuasions are not necessarily trying to take advantage of someone. In all of these cases, it can be argued that the persuasion is even intended to help the other person (or dog) at least a bit. Maybe a lot.

Persuasion can work for the betterment of one party, both parties, or for the betterment of a mass group; society. We see persuasion at work in trial courts as lawyers persuade the jury of someone's innocence or guilt. We see persuasion at work in politics as leaders persuade us to vote in one direction or another. We see persuasion at work in every single Hollywood blockbuster as the actors persuade us to believe this story is real and aliens have landed. We all use persuasion every day whether we are doing it with an artful skill or sloppily and without focus. Persuasion is not automatically corrupt. It's just leading others to believe something that suits us. And maybe them. This is just one of the many tactics we use to communicate.

Manipulation takes it a step further and we often see that manipulation goes hand in hand with persuasion. They just naturally go together like ice cream and cake. Manipulation is the art of changing something for one's own benefit.

Here, we see the intention intensify. Now we are saying that manipulation is most often for one's own benefit. If there is a shared mass benefit to the scenario, it is a side product of the true intention to make the change for oneself.

But is manipulation, with its less selfless intention, a corrupt action? Still no. While it certainly doesn't take much imagination to conjure an example of very corrupt use of manipulation, it does not assume manipulation is evil.

Manipulation is an artful way of pulling at the strings

of a situation to get what you want. There is no more evil in this than in the everyday attempt to survive. If there were no individuals manipulating the edges of the boxes we find ourselves in, there may be no world wide web, no cell phones, no airplanes. I guarantee you manipulation was implemented somewhere along the way by Robert Kahn, Vint Cerf, Martin Cooper, and the Wright brothers.

Perhaps it's in describing it as an art where manipulation starts to look bad. The artful use of it makes it sound and feel like its a trick to pull the wool over one's eyes. It sounds like an intentional deception.

But where do we draw the line? When does the negativity of manipulation stop coming from the use of manipulation and start reflecting the poor judgment and lack of self-preservation as the true culprit? Is it my fault for persuading you or your fault for being persuaded? Am I doing such a terrible thing by persuading you to choose the thing you didn't know you wanted? There is a simple guideline that can be used to measure the level of corruption in your persuasive and manipulative actions. It comes down to this: are you getting the person to do things they want to do? Or, are you getting the person to do things they do not want to do? Play with it long enough and this guideline looks grey and blurry, too.

If I'm so artfully adept at manipulation, it would not be difficult for me to manipulation the circumstance enough to feel justified for my actions in my own eyes. You may be deceptive and secretive to those around you, but ultimately, you cannot lie to yourself. You know if you're using persuasion in a corrupt way or not. With this in mind, there are actually many ways persuasion is used for the benefit of therapists and patients alike, the benefit of parent and child alike. It will be up to you to decide if your natural use of persuasion and/or manipulation will be corrupt or not. It will be up to you to decide if the persuasive tactics used on you or your loved ones are a natural communication or coercion.

Varieties of Persuasive Conversation

If you intend to be skillful at reading others and persuading them, you should be aware of the variety of conversational arenas in which you'll find yourself by deliberate or circumstantial means. It's valuable to gain familiarity with all of these types of persuasive communication whether for your own use or your own protection.

Reverse Psychology

This tactic of persuasion is another we hear so often in media and movies. We are overburdened with examples of this all around us. We see entertainment rife with relatable examples of parents implementing reverse psychology to get their children to act a certain way or complete a task. An example of this might be a father of two siblings on the birthday of the younger sibling. The older sibling has not yet given a present to the birthday sibling. The father might suggest this is the case because the older sibling is selfish, stingy, and greedy and doesn't really love the younger sibling. Thus, the older sibling buys and presents a gift to the younger sibling. This is the result the father wanted all along.

Why did this work? People like to believe they are in control of themselves and their situations. When the father, or someone, proposes the challenge that they are not truly in control of themselves, the person immediately wants to change this, regardless of whether the action originally goes against their desires or not.

Another example of reverse psychology could be right here under your nose. I would suggest that you probably won't go review this book online. It's likely because you are too lazy, lack accountability, or didn't finish reading the book well enough to actually review it. I know it's too difficult for you to take two minutes to produce comprehensive, honest feedback. You don't need to worry about leaving a review, no matter how much this information has helped you. It's too hard for you. Someone else will do it.

Deception

To deceive someone is not necessarily to lie. It's easy enough for me to deceive you without stating any untruth. Deception is a cunning way in which information is presented, truth or not, in a way that persuades the listener to think and feel a certain way about that information and the inferences that can be made from that information.

I can deceive without lying but I cannot lie without deceiving. The trick in a successful deception is to trot out information that will support your case (whether or not it is factual) and apply language artfully in an attempt to make someone feel a particular emotion or agree with a particular line of thinking. Liars can often justify their actions in this way. It is important to pay attention to the words that are spoken and how they are spoken in order to get the truth.

A great example of this is something we see every day. When you visit the grocery store to buy some beef for burgers, you see a sticker with a claim: All natural, organic beef. The sticker doesn't trot out all the information, it's deceptive. It does tell you the beef is all natural organic. It doesn't tell you that is typically but not always the case. That beef might be made with three organically-fed cattle and one old toxic-ridden cow. The sticker doesn't offer all the facts and information— just the ones that will best serve the image they try to maintain. Deceptive.

Mind games

Arguably, mind games begin to cross into the nefarious dark because they are almost always used for the intent and benefit of the manipulator and teeter on whether these games coerce the subject in some way.

We very often see mind games played in romantic relationships and family relationships. This could be due to the wealth of resource knowledge you may have known someone for a long time, as opposed to just meeting them today. That's not to say you cannot play mind games with folks you just meet. This is sometimes used by street performers and magicians. But it's much more common to hear about and experience mind games within established relationships.

When someone uses mind games such as projecting, guilt-tripping, withholding affection, and gaslighting on another individual, it's hard to defend these tactics as positive persuasion. Projecting, for example, is not a heinous crime but it's certainly not a help to anyone but yourself to assume another individual feels the way you feel. This is typically a sign of self-centeredness and disregard for the feelings of others. When you begin to use this behavior to get what you want, it falls on the blurry line of manipulating others to do what they do not want to do. Very similarly, guilt-tripping, withholding affection, and gaslighting are not the very worst psychological tactics one could use but they are definitely on that blurry line. Can these tactics be used in a more positive way? Absolutely. It's possible that an individual may employ these tactics to mitigate the psychological abuse being dealt with them by another. These tactics could become coping mechanisms under the right circumstance. It's important to keep in mind that by and large, these kinds of behaviors may seem tempting to get what you want but if you examine the entire situation and the consequences of these tactics, you may find using them is not in alignment with what you really want at all.

Brainwashing

We move even closer to the dark side of psychology when we discuss brainwashing and mind control. This tactic is difficult to defend. The vast majority of examples of brainwashing and mind control are coercion. It seems obvious to say if the individual really wanted the outcome, the brainwashing would not be unnecessary. By definition, brainwashing applies systematic and forcible means to persuade someone into a new set of beliefs. It's the systematic and forcible approach to persuasion that truly puts this technique on the dark side. A compulsory indoctrination (social, political, religious, or otherwise) beliefs is coercive. When we hear brainwashing, we think perhaps of Prisoners of War and cult followers who may be subjected to this tactic and those like in order to break down will and identity of the individual.

Beyond these dramatic cases of brainwashing, a shady but less nefarious version confronts us: subliminal messages. Not only does media report on these stories but marketing employs these tactics constantly. Remember the song that praises Satan when you listen to it backwards or upside down? The media hypes examples of subliminal messaging like this (by preying on our fear of being subliminally controlled).

A much less vicious example is the recent change of

Wendy's fast food logo. The new icon cleverly uses a bit of subliminal messaging right below the friendly face of Wendy. Wendy's shirt collar is drawn in such a way that it depicts the scrolled word "Mom". This evokes a sense of home-cooked goodness when we see it. As you might have figured out, too, it utilizes anchoring to link that home-cooked goodness to the logo and to the excitement and satisfaction we feel when ordering and opening our Wendy's bag of food.

Hypnosis

Let's take it back around to the light side of psychology. Hypnosis is a perfect transition for this. There are plenty of scary examples of hypnosis in media. The creepy man who makes a slave of the object of his affection. The political leader who changes someone into a Manchurian candidate. The trauma victim who goes into a hypnotic trance and gets stuck there.

It's not a lie that hypnosis can also be used in a coercive way but it is definitely the minority example. Hypnosis, in the broad and boundless sense, is applied much more regularly in the case of patient and therapist, client and coach, professional and apprentice, and the like. Hypnosis is structured in psychotherapy and in fact, many of the works and technique produced by Milton Erickson are the foundation for the therapeutic hypnosis that is practiced today. Hypnosis is a fast and effective tool to use in supplement when trying to modify a behavior in oneself, such as smoking, or overeating. Hypnosis is a routine was to bring the self or the client back to that highly suggestible alpha or theta state to implant the possibility (and strategy) for the desired outcome. For example, we can consider a Harvard student has a rigorous exam coming up in a month. Hypnosis would be a very effective tactic to supplement with study and practice. Essentially, hypnosis can help to make studying easier for the student, more exciting, less exhausting, and more rewarding.

Persuasive Language

It's not what you say and it's not how you say it. It's both. People are reading you and you are reading people, both in terms of body language and actual language, every day. To be your most persuasive, you should practice deliberate verbal language and deliberate body language, both, and together.

If you don't practice either of them, your speech may be less cohesive and easy to relate to. Your body language might inform your audience that you are nervous, unprepared, and unauthoritative. This might influence the audience, consciously or subconsciously, to feel a certain way about you that may not be beneficial to you.

If you practice one without the other, congratulations, you are already a step ahead. Like many of us, you would probably practice the speaking language but not body language. Maybe because you're unaware of body language, or you think others are unaware of it. However, a recent study claims that job interviewers take about 38% of their insights and feelings about an interviewee from body language. The actual words only account for about 8% of the interviewers' insights and takeaways. So maybe you've practiced your speech a few times in the shower. You've carefully selected some of your words. You've organized your ideas to drive your point home. But your body language still reveals to the audience that you feel nervous, underprepared, lacking confidence.

So why not get it all right and practice both the speaking language you will use to persuade your audience but also the deliberate body language you will use to persuade them. This way, your words communicate clearly what you want your audience to consider, how you want them to feel, and what you want them to do. Your body language communicates an air of professionalism and authority to anyone consciously paying attention. For those audience members who are not deliberately taking into account your body language may just find that they relate better to you, feel you are speaking directly to them or just really dig your vibe, even though they aren't sure why. You've used your body language in conjunction with your speaking language to build a rapport with your audience and to persuade them toward your goal.

Persuasive Speaking

To perform your most persuasive speaking, there is an often overlooked step that should never be skipped. Warm up your instrument. You never see musicians step out on stage without warming up and tuning their instruments. It's silly for you to try and be your most persuasive without warming up your voice. Speakers, lawyers, politicians, trainers, actors all use voice coaches to maximize their potential to persuade their audience.

Take the time to practice warming up your voice. If you're a frequent speaker, you may want to consider developing a quick couple of effective warm-up exercises you can do before you speak. Record yourself and listen back, or speak aloud in front of a friend and play with different kinds of speaking. Experiment with your timbre and register, your notes and prosody, your pacing and pitch, and your silence. Studies suggest the most well-liked voice sounds are lower pitches with soft and velvety tones that speak slowly and allow the listener to digest and consider information. These can all be used to draw emphasis, create an emotion or response, and to bypass the critical mind and allow for imagination of possibilities to begin.

Four Persuasive Phrases

There are infinite phrases and combinations of words that can be extremely persuasive in the right scenarios but there are four key phrases that most persuasive speakers will agree are versatile fast and effective.

"Imagine…"

Imagine is a magic word that can lead the listener to a point where they must imagine a scenario you give them, in order to understand what you're saying. But the word "imagine" can be used in so many ways to draw out the listener's creativity. When using the word "imagine", it's often paired with sensory perceptions as we saw with neuro-linguistic programming. Next time someone tells you they just can't do it. They've tried and they just can't. See what happens when you ask them to imagine what would happen if they did do it. Pay attention to whether you actually got the person to start thinking about doing and completing the thing as a possibility.

"If…"

If is another magic word that can be used like "imagine". "If" gets the listener to break from critical logical thought, suspend their own limiting beliefs for a moment, and engage the imagination in another possibility; one where the goal is accomplished or the behavior is changed. By working through the if/then scenario in their imagination, the listener has unintentionally expanded their own internal map of reality. There are possibilities recorded on the map that indicate the goal is impossible, except for that one time when, at least in imagination, the goal was possible. Practice this imagination long enough and your map changes in a big way. A little stream, that used to never even be there, has now become a river through what used to be a limitation and boundary.

"Either, or"

The "either, or" phrase is a great one to use in a sales scenario or even a therapeutic one. By implementing the "either, or" phrase, you are asking your listener to picture two scenarios, which you've already narrowed down to the choice that is unwanted, and the choice that is wanted. For example, a weight coach says to her client, "Bob, either you continue eating and living this way and feeling unhealthy or you can make these small diet adjustments and gradually live a healthier life." Bob now visualizes each scenario and one undoubtedly sounds better than the other, persuading him to choose the latter. Another easily applied example of this might be a telemarketer setting appointments for field reps. The telemarketer does not ask, "Do you want to meet with ou rep?" Instead, the telemarketer asks, "Do you want to meet with our rep Tuesday or Friday?" Now the listener is choosing between one or the other, and not about whether they even want to see a rep.

"I need your help"

Don't be afraid to ask for help, even if you don't need it. Asking someone to help you, even if you don't need it, is a powerful tool of persuasion. It incorporates a few tactics into one, very subtly. Asking someone for their help implies that not only are you sure they can help you, but you trust them enough to ask. This ego stroke is often enough to get someone to help or execute a task for you. But if that's not enough, asking for help also puts the other person in the social position of saying no to someone. Often, people don't want to create any uncomfortable confrontation so they will comply. Other times, people will not want to be seen as rude or as a jerk so they will comply and help you. Finally, asking for help can be a setup to a bigger favor you intend to ask down the line. An example of this might be to ask your new acquaintance if you can borrow a dollar for a drink. Of course, you give them back the dollar next time you see each other. But that is a setup scenario, because the next time you see your friend, you're going to ask them for a bigger favor; can I borrow $100? In the mind of your new acquaintance, you've already asked for a favor and kept your integrity so he will be more apt to invest in you and trust you again.

In addition to these four powerful phrases, there are three more tips for practical persuasion that can help increase persuasion when speaking.

The first tip is that your silence is a vacuum that starts at your eyes. Use silence deliberately to accentuate and punctuate important points and emotions. Use silence to make your listener ponder the scenario you've just described. Don't be afraid to implement silence in your speaking and not just in your voice. Silence is most powerful when accompanied by locked eye contact. Lock on and say nothing.

The second time is to whisper. Use the whisper technique in your speaking. It will have to make sense where you use it though or it will seem strange and cause your audience to feel skeptical. Instead of random use, plant a whisper where it works best: the call-to-action. By whispering to your audience or listener, a sense of secrecy and trust immediately exists. Not only is it effective for your rapport but it subliminally conveys a level of urgency and discretion.

The third tip is to refrain from oversimplification. This may not always be the case but when it comes to statistics and figures, people do not like to see a rounded number. Sales increased this month over last month by 23.8%, not by about 20% or about 24%, because in this case, people like to see the more accurate and specific figure. It seems more legitimate and scientific perhaps. It conveys honesty perhaps. You also don't want to confuse people though so keep it within reason. Depending on your overall picture, consider that it will be most valuable to keep your figures one, two, or maybe three places to the right of the decimal. Any more than that and the figure starts to slide back into a skeptical light.

Persuasive Body

Persuasive body language can go a long way and your job as a persuasive speaker is not done until you use these tools and resources, as well. Using your body language is often more effective than the words we use to communicate. Whether we are aware of the body language we are broadcasting or focused on reading the body language of another, attention to these clues is critical.

Next time you're in a situation where persuasive communication is required of you, consider your posture, your stance, and the direction of your shoulders and feet. All of these details are revealing something. Posture, we know, is a very common way that we as humans gauge someone's self-worth and self-confidence. Usually, someone with a slouching posture is less confident than someone who stands tall. Is your stance aggressive, too close, and overbearing? Or maybe it's unintentionally the opposite and you're giving false cues to the other person that you are bored and uninterested in what they have to say. Are your feet crossed? Pointed straight ahead? Toward the door? The direction of your feet and shoulders can communicate whether you are closed off to the person with whom you're speaking or whether you are giving undivided attention or you just can't wait to get to the door and leave.

When in conversation next time, try a laughing attraction. Laugh casually and smile about something you're talking about. As you listen and pay attention when they speak, do they mimic that behavior? Sometimes this cue is so strong it happens immediately. You could, for example, laugh and smile subtly when discussing the sales numbers for the month. If the cue is strong enough, the other person will mimic you immediately, smiling and offering a polite chuckle as well, even if humor has nothing to do with the topic. Don't make it weird though. If you try to pull off a laughing attraction when the conversation is sad for example, you will come across as callous and unsociable.

A similar technique for reading people and building rapport with body language is to mirror an action the other person takes. If the other person pushes her hair back when speaking, you do the same motion. If the other person crosses her arms, cross yours. If the other person speaks with their hands be sure to gesticulate when you speak, too. This is a sign that you are in harmony with the other person. Mirroring the behaviors of others sets up an unconscious bond between the two of you, that you are very much alike, at least, on the internal map of reality where it counts.

There is one more important key to consider when reading the body language of others in order to deliver your most persuasive communication. The key is to assess whether you are talking to a visual person, an auditory person, or a kinesthetic person.

The visual person accounts for about 75% of the people with whom we come in contact. This person thinks mainly in pictures and images. Ideas are saved as visuals in their mind. Visual people even use language that pertains to vision or seeing without even meaning to. "I see what you mean", "Let's keep an eye out", "Watch what happens when I go in there". The visual person usually stands tall with generally good posture. This person, being more concerned with appearance, is typically well-dressed. This individual tends to hold stress in their shoulders, pulling them back a bit. They tend to look up when remembering something and therefore often have developed wrinkles on their forehead. This person will often have thin lips instead of full lips and they love a lot of eye contact. Eye contact with the visual person is important because it helps them gain trust and rapport with you and indicates to them that you are paying attention and interested in what they are saying to you.

The auditory person accounts for about 20% of the people with whom we come in contact. This person thinks in words and sounds. They may not be as well-dressed as the visual person and this is because the visual representation of themselves (and others) is not as important to them as the information shared and derived by sound and the voice. This individual is less likely than the visual person to enjoy making eye contact. They are, however, the type of person who might be clicking their pen, tapping their foot, or drumming the table while they are concentrating and digesting information. These individuals are in effect creating a more memorable and meaningful experience with the information they are receiving because it's being saved in the mind along with sound patterns, which will make it easier for them to recall in the future. Auditory people, like visual people, use language that unintentionally matches their style such as: "I hear what you're saying", or "I like the sound of that".

The kinesthetic person is the hugger. This accounts for only 5% of the people with whom we come in contact. They want to get to know you by feeling you and feeling the vibe you give off when they are near to you. This person also loves to physically connect in conversation even in plutonic ways, such as a touch on the arm or shoulder. These individuals are dressed for comfort 100% and tend to have the fuller lips the visual person lacks. If you're not a person who likes to touch but you still don't want to break a good rapport with this type of person, you can implement a point of contact for them that you are comfortable with. Maybe a handshake will suffice for you instead of a hug. The kinesthetic person speaks with matching language as well as the visual and the auditory individuals and you may catch them saying something like, "I don't feel that was the right choice".

Next time you are in a room of people, especially if you don't know them as well as you know your friends, observe these individuals and see if you can pick out who is the visual person, who is the auditory person, and who is the hugger. Which one are you?

Dangerous Manipulation

Now we've learned about the subtle differences in persuasion and manipulation. You can persuade someone to think, believe, or act in accordance with that which you want and we've seen this is not necessarily a bad or deceitful behavior. A consumer may want a lawnmower but they are actually looking for, in need of, someone that can persuade them toward one brand and away from another. Ultimately, they do want a lawnmower to rid themselves of the problem of long grass in the yard but they want to be given some choices. More than 70% of the time, an individual will check online for reviews of an item before making a decision to buy it or not. These reviews are a method of persuasion that we have actually come to rely on.

We've also learned that very often, manipulation can go hand in hand with persuasion, but manipulation takes it a step further, seeking to actually change something about their environment or the people in it, in order to bring about a certain outcome. Again, when used in a productive way, manipulation can be a legitimate and effective tool. Consider the activist who is fed up with the lack of a local leash law. Every time this individual is out and about in town, she sees dogs roaming free on the sides of roads. The activist is concerned for the safety of the animals, the drivers, and the pedestrians who may be fearful of dogs. This activist uses the power of manipulation to change the beliefs of the lawmakers in the jurisdiction. Through manipulation, the activist changes the local environment so that now in her town, dogs must be leashed unless in a fenced zone meant for accommodating dogs (like a dog park). This use of manipulation has been a constructive one.

We've also compared the similarities and differences between persuasion, manipulation, and coercion, and it is here that we dive a bit deeper next. Manipulation can very easily be a slippery slope down to coercion. Individuals that practice coercion to achieve their goals can easily become predators, quenching their corrupt thirst on the weaker targets around them. It's imperative that we take extra time to delineate between constructive manipulation and dangerous manipulation. You don't want to act in a malicious way within your community. You don't want to accidentally give the impression that you are a subversive and amoral member of your community. Least of all, do you want to be a target for a manipulative individual or a victim of their manipulation?

Predators

What does a predator look like? Can you tell by the

way they stand? Could a predator be the last person to give me a sales pitch? Could it be my cab driver? Could it be the internet troll that won't let the topic go? There is definitely a level of at least attempted manipulation at work in every one of these day-to-day examples. Truthfully, a predator could be any one of these people or it might even be someone that hits closer to home. It could be your neighbor, your uncle, your son's teacher. Predators come in all shapes and forms, all levels of affluence, any race or sex. Some predators are very well aware of themselves and conduct themselves as a normal trusting person on the exterior. Ted Bundy was generally thought to be an attractive individual who spoke intellectually. Much of the reason it took so long to identify him as a serial killer was that he happened to be so acutely aware of how he was broadcasting, and how others were broadcasting, that he did an impeccable job of disguising himself as a normal healthy human. Traits of an actual predator can be more subtle or well-hidden. The behavior patterns of these individuals are what serve as the best clues. As we focus for a moment on the more dangerous manipulators try to be aware of the behavior patterns you'll want to watch out for as you go into the world with your newfound tools of persuasion.

Alfred Adler points out in his later works that the more extreme a feeling of inferiority is for the individual, the more extreme measures will be taken to gain superiority over another. An extreme feeling of inferiority is something to watch out for. This may be hard to trace at first because so many are good at hiding this trait. But pay attention and you will find all the little opportunities that the individual takes to define themselves, consciously or unconsciously, as the victor, the most superior. The first crack in the picture is usually found in the way the individual will talk about others. If the individual often talks as if another is below them, it could be a sign.

Dangerous manipulators will use fear as a base for their victims. This could come in the form of a fearful possible outcome (financial ruin), a physical threat (rape), or perhaps the fear of having one's social status destroyed (blackmail). The coercive individual knows what we know; fear is an effect that almost every organism uses for operation in the day to day world. The malicious individual latches onto this fear and uses it against another.

The internet is rife with cyber predators in the form of internet trolls, data criminals, cyber bullies, stalkers, sex predators, cyber terrorists, serial killers, you name it. While the internet has leveled the playing field for communications, education, and business, it's also done the same for predators and criminals. It's easier than ever for personal information to be stolen and sold online. Credit card hacks, stolen identities, drug laundering, there is no limit to the plethora of new cybercrime games criminals can play. From the safety of their own home, child predators can learn everything they need to know and use it against a target to manipulate and coerce them. Predators are a category of predator all their own. This person engages in the exploitation and victimization of their prey mostly through the internet or telecommunications. This behavior is exceptionally dangerous because the perpetrator has had countless time behind the screen getting away with what they want to get away with in reality. This only heightens the individual's sense of superiority and intensifies their desires. If you recall our review of the Dark Singularity at the start of this book, this is the category where you will find these types of personalities.

There are other behavioral patterns that predators share. They tend to prey on people with a need. If they are locked on a target without a strong need, they will try to use manipulation and mind games to create one. This is why malicious individual tries to target individuals with low self-esteem, low self-worth, or a lack of confidence. These individuals, it is assumed, will be easier to exploit and control because their need for acceptance and attention is greater than someone with a high level of confidence and self-worth.

Manipulative people will use mixed signals (another mind game) to attempt to control their target. For instance, a manipulative person might send you a text message gushing over being with you, but then that person will go silent on you for days. You will be left to wonder if you've done something wrong to make the person go from loving you to ignoring you.

Manipulators will sometimes build contrasting qualities in appearance to make themselves seem more dynamic and mysterious. For example, a very muscular male bodybuilder with an incredibly masculine form might also have a man-bun hairstyle and visit the yoga studio to accentuate the more feminine side of himself. Whether he likes the hair or the yoga at all is not the point for this person. The image it conveys is the goal. Along the same lines, this manipulative person may build social media profiles for themselves for the sole purpose of broadcasting what they want you to think they are, what they want you to think their life is. These broadcasts, again, may have hints of a superiority complex within them.

A manipulator is not afraid to inflict at least mental and emotional pain onto another and in fact, looks for ways to do that so it can be used to control the target at a later time. A typical example might be a manipulative girlfriend has a boyfriend who is short and blond. She deliberately, but subtly, will make sure the boyfriend understands her favorite type of male is a tall dark-haired one. This might just be in a passing comment while you're watching the new Captain America movie together. The boyfriend may not even pick up on it right away. But the criticism has been locked into the boyfriend's subconscious and the manipulative girlfriend knows it. She waits patiently for the seeds of insecurity to grow. She will look for just the right time to reference this again, to make the boyfriend feel inferior when it is beneficial for her. "If you don't want to buy me dinner, then let's just go home and watch Captain America."

A manipulator doesn't mind showering their target with gifts. This builds up the manipulator in the mind of the victim and makes them seem more credible and caring. In reality, the manipulator is showering the victim with gifts and adulation because they intend to take it from you later. If you obey and go along with what the manipulator wants, they will spoil you. If you show resistance or your own opposing will in some way, the manipulator will suddenly become agitated and angry and will only treat you harshly and with cruelty when you do.

Subtle and low key is usually the key to getting into the subconscious, whether for productive or nefarious purposes. Manipulators may seem like they are giving you their full attention, and in a way, they are. But it's not the way you probably think. The manipulator is an excellent listener when they want to be because they are listening for any information that can be used to bring about their desired outcome. Is that person really so interested in what you have to say about a book you read five years ago, or are they playing you?

Prey

The victims that predators prey upon is probably not that hard to deduce on your own. Naturally, the predator seeks out the weak ones, the ones who are unable to defend themselves, or unable to know any better.

This is the victimization we see with manipulative individuals and predators. Though a victim can just as easily be any race, age, sex, creed, or social status, they are most usually those who cannot defend themselves. In our society, this often breaks down to children, teens, women, addicts, homeless individuals, mentally ill or mentally challenged individuals, and the elderly. This is especially the case with internet predators. So much personal risk is removed for the online predator, but so much personal risk is there for the victim. By now, we've all heard of the internet and phone scams that target the elderly and those with poor credit. The scammer claims to be a government body of some kind, often the IRS, and calls or emails the victim to demand a payment method for an outstanding tax or bill. Scared by the threat of warrants and jail time, the victim concedes and provides a credit card number. The scammer takes the victim's information and money and disappears. There never was a real outstanding bill, or government representative, or warrant, or jail time. Another such crime is targeted at older generations of people who may not be as internet savvy as their younger counterparts. In this scam, the manipulator emails the older person and threatens that they have hacked into the older person's computer. From the computer, they retrieved web camera images of the older person visiting porn sites and pleasuring themselves. The manipulator threatens that these images will be dispersed to all contacts in the person's computer or profiles unless a price is paid. Of course, there is no hack, and there is no webcam image. Just a scared and embarrassed individual who does not want to be humiliated. It's a blackmail scam that has increased in frequency in the last couple of years.

In addition to the usual target traits that signify weakness and need, the manipulator looks for other aspects of life that may hold the possibility of something for them to exploit or use as leverage. The manipulator may notice that a target is having a rough time in their romantic relationship and that could be a mark. Just as easily, the manipulator might pick a target because they are in the midst of a perfect relationship. There are plenty of ways for a manipulator to use that to their advantage as well.

The faith and spiritual or religious convictions one holds can also make for an easy target. Doubly tempting if the person with faith is also down on their luck. They want to keep their faith and believe things will get better and this desperation can be used and exploited by someone meaning to use someone to their advantage. On the other side of that, if the down-on-their-luck individual is losing faith, the master manipulator might step in and offer a whole new set of beliefs to save the day. The persuasive schemer might suggest that the values and beliefs once held by the faithful are no longer serving. Perhaps they would consider a new path. This is a common gateway for cult members to be brought in, isolated, and brainwashed.

As we've mentioned before, victims of manipulation and coercion tend to be those who have low self-esteem and low self-worth, and those who project a low level of self-confidence. Even if you have not achieved a high self-worth yet, you now know how to project your voice and your body as though you do. This alone could protect you or your loved ones from a manipulator.

Additional Traits to Read or Broadcast

You now have a comprehensive understanding of the basics of reading those around you. Likewise, you have a solid grasp on how to use your speech and your body to broadcast in your own favor. Here are just a few more traits from which to gain (or give) insights.

Eye contact can be a sign of an auditory or kinesthetic person (rather than a visual one), and this is nothing to be worried about but an aversion to eye contact may also be a sign of deception or lying. Consider the context and the other language communications you're picking up from the person.

Eyebrows are a clue on comfort level. Relaxed eyebrows are a sign of comfort. One raised eyebrow is a sign of interest or skepticism. Both raised eyebrows is a sign that the person is experiencing surprise, worry, or fear.

Lips are a trickier one to read and the takeaway can be rather vague, but typically those with fat, full, lips are free-spirited, childlike, and even immature. Those with thin lips are perceived as more responsible and mature.

Though we might not mean to, we do read into the shape of peoples' lips. Next time you're in a crowd, take note of whether individuals have thin or full lips and whether that trait seems to match up with other inferences you may be able to draw out of their body language and speech.

Smiles can be very revealing but not to unmask who will be a nice friend for you, rather, to find out who is a liar. When a person exhibits a normal healthy happy smile, the eyes are involved in that expression. The individual's lips will smile but the eyes will, too. Smiling eyes have small crinkles at the outer corners of the eyes, something that is a very tricky muscle movement to fake deliberately. Attempt to fake them on your own face. You will see that trying to fake the eye crinkles looks even more bizarre than a liar's empty eyes.

The side glance is a subconscious movement that often reveals that the individual is nervous or uncomfortable and wants to escape the situation.

Nodding is an interesting trait to observe because we (at least in the Western world) tend to use nods to mean a variety of things from mundane to sinister. The trick here, like eye contact, is in the context. Is the person nodding to hurry you along in conversation? Are they nodding out of concern and care for your emotions? Or is the individual nodding because they just agree with you? Consider other communicative information available to you in that instance to help make a determination.

People tend to touch their jaw or chin with their hand when they are making decisions in their mind but because this is a common theme in media from cartoons to Shakespeare, people also make this gesture when they want you to think they are making a decision or consideration. For this reason, you should pay extra close attention. Is the person also looking down and to the side or are they looking at you or straight ahead? A decision-making gesture with a glance that points down and to the side is a genuine decision or consideration being made. If the person is looking at you or looking straight ahead, the chances of that being genuine are low.

A parent has a unique trait for reading body language, particularly if it is the parent of a new baby. If the parent is holding their baby cradled in their less dominant arm (usually the left arm) then the parent is not showing signs of stress. If the parent is holding the baby cradled in their dominant arm (usually the right arm) the parent is showing signs of stress. The stress may be related to parenting but it may not.

Crossed arms or legs are a strong subconscious sign that the person exhibiting this is closed off to the person or situation they are facing. This may be out of an exaggerated need to protect oneself in general but it could also be a sign that they are specifically untrusting of the person to whom they are conversing.

Positive Manipulation

Before we complete our look at the overall traits and behaviors of manipulators, we turn back again from the dark side of psychology and rejoin the light. It was mentioned earlier; not all manipulation is negative. Manipulation is a natural mechanism for us. Manipulation can help to strengthen communities. Manipulation can be used to raise awareness. Manipulation can be used to raise funds for a beneficial goal. Like all tools at our disposal, manipulation can be used in a negative way, or a positive one.

Hiding in the cracks is a powerful lesson about manipulation and why it's so wonderful—hiding in the cracks, specifically. Think of those little creased white paper cups you get at the burger restaurant. They are small folded waxy paper cups we usually fill with ketchup or ranch sauce. They don't fit all that much sauce so you probably end up grabbing several and filling them.

But were you aware that if you unfold the cup, the creases open to reveal more than double the space for filling ketchup? If you just tug at the edges, you can use one little cup for three times the fries. Yet it's rare to see anyone tug at the cup. Everyone just has a tray of 10 cups. They saw someone else do it that way and never questioned it. Don't feel bad if you're still a 10-cupper and not a crease-tugger. That's all changing for you. But this is an excellent example for you about why you should not fear your utilization of manipulation. The cup hasn't even reached half its potential until you tug at its creases and open it up. How many other things in your life have creases you're missing?

Without a bit of questioning, without a bit of rebellion, without a bit of manipulating the objects in your environment, the potentials would be lost. Do not squander this tool but rather, nurture it and learn to use your powers for good; your good and the good of others. Don't be afraid to tug and poke. Use the cunning skills you've developed and look closer. Look deeper. Look for the creases you can tug at to get the full potential of what you want. You'll enjoy the extra ketchup.

Practical Application

You've come a long way in learning about persuasive communications. The previous chapters have readied you. All you have left to do now is practice regularly. These skills can be yours and serve you the way they serve others every day.

By now you understand that utilizing persuasion and manipulation can be a very positive thing. These are natural behaviors and part of the grand repertoire of language and communication. You should just as soon abandon the use of the alphabet. You can continue through your life knowing you could tug at the creases for more ketchup but you don't. Or, you could tug. Imagine what your life could be if you just learned to implement a few effective modes of communication to get what you want. What if you asked for a raise and didn't even need to negotiate because your boss was happy to do it? You're selling it or getting sold.

You know now that there are times in life that communication tactics like lying, manipulating, and persuading are going to be necessary. It is much better to know how to use these instruments responsibly. Now you're aware of how to read others and what it means. You can protect against predatory behaviors from others. You can get extra ketchup. You can get people to agree with you and want the outcome you want. There are just two last critical techniques that will come in pretty handy.

How to Lie

Surely you've told at least one lie in your lifetime but are you a good liar or did the person see right through you? Lying, while generally frowned upon, is actually another unavoidable mechanism for communication. Whether you've been the spider or the fly, in a big web or a modest one, you know that lying is a part of life. Sometimes a little lie helps to spare hurt feelings or hurry along with a task. Sometimes lies have good intentions but the plan backfires. Save yours from backfiring by learning and practicing these skills for constructive lying.

Try paltering first. This is referred to commonly (especially by politicians) as the ethical lie. This would be practicing deception in your speech without technically lying. An example of this might be when a mother asks her teenage son if he took $200 from her purse. The son replies, "I don't have any of your money." This is not a lie. If she checks, the mother will find that her son indeed does not have any of her money. What was not said, and thus deceptive, is that the son does not have her money because he did take it and already spent it.

Believe your own lies if you can and enjoy the process of sharing them. Bad liars try to get the lie over with as quickly as they can and this almost always leads to a messy lie that backfires.

Base your lie in some truth so that it's easier for you to justify to yourself and believe. This also makes it easier to remember your lie. If you're lying to someone you know, like a boss, keeping your lie based in some truth, especially a truth your boss is aware of, it will be more easily accepted. For example, if you're not feeling well on Thursday and your boss has witnessed this or even commented on it, it will make lying about not coming in on Friday all the easier to pitch to your boss and easier for your boss to accept.

Keep your story simple. Sometimes people think that by including all manner of extra details makes the story more believable and real. However, it tends to have the opposite effect. Typically a truthful story does not include all manner of extra details. It only includes the details that are pertinent to the story. When you start to include random details, people become more suspicious of it. When children lie, they often make this mistake. As adults, we remember that and feel skeptical when it happens.

Don't overact. Remember subtly is your friend. If your lie comes with exaggerated gesticulation or drama, it doesn't sound like the truth. It sounds like you're working extra hard to cover up the truth. For example, the same Thursday afternoon in the office and your boss walks through. You make an extra effort to cough and wheeze. A few hours later, your boss comes to speak with you and you do the same thing and fake a terrible cough. This will catch your boss as rather unusual and when you call in on Friday morning, your fake cough will suddenly seem like an obvious deception.

Keep your lies in check. Knowing how to lie effectively doesn't mean you should tell lies without regard. Being a good liar means being a responsible liar. If you can tell the truth, you should. It's easier for you and it's easier to believe you when you do actually use a lie tactic. Liars are often caught because they tell so many lies to so many people that their stories are no longer consistent. Lying well means lying less.

The Person with the Most Control

There is one secret key left for you to learn if you want to be a productive persuader. This is the number one practice that ensures you are the person in the room with the most control and the most confidence. This number one practice is so obvious that it's also the most overlooked. Everyone thinks they know how to do this already. Breathe. But understand this, it's not just remembering to breathe. That's pretty good advice but it seems like you've got that one down. Breathe strategically. Use a regulated breath.

Take your thumb and put it to your chest, just below where an underwire of a bra would be. Press in gently with your thumb. Now, take a deep breath. You will feel your diaphragm pushing back on your thumb. Put your hands around your chest (your diaphragm stretches around you). Breathe in and out again and you will feel your diaphragm at work. There is a reason that stage actors have diaphragm exercises with their voice coaches. The diaphragm holds a great resource of power for you because it can be used to regulate your breath. When your breath is slow and steady, you appear to be in the most control. You appear to be the least disrupted or upset, or worried. You appear to be the one who has it most together. This appearance, whether entirely true or not, it is your key to being the most confident; the calmest and collected. Others will naturally look to you for guidance or help.

One final thought when it comes to using your breath to gain control of yourself and your reactions: know when to close your mouth. When we speak, we pass our thoughts on our breath. We don't speak as we inhale; we speak as we exhale. Train your body to close your mouth when you inhale and open it to speak on the exhale. This is another sure sign of the well-regulated breath of a confident person.

Practice, Test, and Measure

In just this short time you've come to be familiar with which techniques to use, when, and why, if you want to capture someone's attention. Once you have their attention, you know how to hold it and how to access their imagination in order to plant powerful suggestions. You know which types of body language tell you to stay away from someone or when to move closer. You have seen how to apply these techniques responsibly in your personal and professional life. You've learned how to get the outcomes you want from yourself and from others. Take a moment to congratulate yourself on all you've just learned!

You just learned about:

- Adler, Paulhus, Erickson, Bandler, and Grinder

- What makes psychology dark

- Four dark personalities to be aware of

- Traits of manipulators and victims

- Three central concepts of NLP

- Four pillars of NLP

- How we get manipulated by fear

- Social manipulation and mass manipulation

- How to customize the internal map of reality for yourself and others

- How to use modeling, anchoring, and reframing

- The difference between persuasion, manipulation, and coercion

- Manipulative tactics like deception, mind games, brainwashing, and hypnosis

- How to manipulate and persuade safely with body language and speech

- How to induce a confusion state and a trance state

- Sounds and expressions to be aware of in yourself and others

- Four persuasive phrases

- How to use your body, posture, stance, and laugh to persuade

- Mirroring to persuade

- Visual, auditory, and kinesthetic learners

- Dangerous manipulation and predators

- How to use and read eye contact, eyebrows, lips, and smile,

- How stressed parents hold babies

- How to lie

- How to have the most control in the room

- The power of positive manipulation

Do you feel better about what you now know? If

you've learned new information you know will help you, take a moment to provide feedback for this book online so that it might help someone else in the same shoes you used to be in.

You have mastered the class. Now, put it to work. Each day, every place you go, pay attention to others. How are they carrying themselves? Thin lips or full? The visual thinker or the kinesthetic one? The more you practice this, the easier it is and the more adept you become. Soon, reading the silent broadcasts of others will be as easily seen as what they wear.

Pay attention to your own broadcasting. Are there areas you'd like to improve? Get an idea for what you'd like to be broadcasting and how you could change it. Maybe it's your posture or your eye contact. Practice how you'd like it to be, in the mirror, to yourself, on camera, to a friend. Finally, to the world. The more you practice it, the stronger it gets and the better you are at it.

When you're comfortable reading others and using your own body language in a persuasive way, select a couple of other persuasive techniques you'd like to try. Think of a good place to test them out and put yourself there. Test them.

Don't stop at testing them out. This isn't a casual application. You should know by now that persuasion and neuro-linguistic programming are a highly structured and formulaic application of communication. Keep a journal of your results each time you test. Consider what you wanted the outcome to be and how close you got to that goal. It will be equally as beneficial to record details like your environment, your mood, the mood, and the broadcast of the people in your environment, other influences, unplanned events, and so forth. While this sounds like a bit of effort, it pays off. You'll be surprised at what patterns become visible to you and how useful that information can be. Especially true for the motivated learner who wants to ramp up fast and master the process.

Make time for analysis. Now that you've diligently recorded your results, don't blow off studying it. There is a valuable insight into the analysis process which allows you to tweak a process or improve a plan. Look over your progress at least once every quarter and see what you can take away to improve the next quarter's progress.

You can practice and master your skills in everyday places like:

- Grocery line
- Customer support call
- Email chain
- Team meeting
- Commute
- Restaurant
- Phone call

- Town meeting
- Real estate bid
- Doctor's office

In addition to the everyday interactions you're going to have anyway, consider planning (manipulating) some of your own. You can set the stage and play the part. Take any day of the week and put on your best, finest, clothing or suit. Spruce yourself up. Find the classiest hotel in your area and go there. The most expensive one. Go inside and head to the hotel's restaurant, bar, or cafe. The choice is yours. Maybe bring an intentional book with you, or your laptop. Settle in with a drink. Read the room. What types of people are coming and going, and staying? See whether you're able to get someone to come over and talk to you or if you'd be welcome to strike up a conversation with them. Test your skills in this deliberate, but spontaneous playing field. Record your results.

Conclusion

Thank you for making it through to the end of *Manipulation and Persuasion by NLP*. You've met your goal to gain this knowledge and insight. You will surely take the next step to activate your powers of observation. Each day, you will become stronger and faster with these observations. Before long, you will naturally find yourself working off of these indicators and communicating with others in a more effective and persuasive way. Others will be drawn to you as an authority they can trust. Those around you will feel they really connect with you even though it may only be the first time meeting you. As you gain experience and confidence with this new information, you will find ways to utilize it in your everyday (and extraordinary) situations to get what you want and help others. It's amazing to think if you've already come this far; where you might be in another 30 days.

Can you imagine standing in front of your colleagues, finally able to deliver your amazing idea eloquently? Finally, you are able to get those around you to understand you better. Finally, everyone will see you know what you're doing and they will naturally want to follow your lead and make you happy. What if you were able to navigate the awkward social situations and tense moments better than anyone in the room? Think of the kind of person you'd be.

Let's hope *Manipulation and Persuasion by NLP* has been (and continues to be) informative and practical in your personal and professional life. You've been provided with all of the tools you need to achieve your goals whatever they may be. The world is your playground. If you put your imagination to it, there is an opportunity in every single interaction you have. Use every resource.

316

www.ingramcontent.com/pod-product-compliance
Lightning Source LLC
Chambersburg PA
CBHW031050250726
48655CB00004B/1379